GW01339850

*The Extraordinary Life of Ana M. Young*

# Miracle of Mom

*Catherine Anne Young*

# Miracle of Mom
## The Extraordinary Life of Ana M. Young
### Catherine Anne Young

Copyright © by Catherine Anne Young

All rights reserved. No part of this book may be reproduced or transmitted in any form or by any means, electronic or mechanical, including photocopying, recording, or by any information storage or retrieval system, without written permission from the author or the publisher, except for the inclusion of brief quotations in a review.

## Published by Cincinnati Book Publishing
www.CincyBooks.com

Anthony W. Brunsman, president
Sue Ann Painter, executive editor
Michelle Kallmeyer, associate editor
Greg Eckel, design

ISBN: 979-8-9870255-0-5

Library of Congress Control Number: 2022951679

Printed in the United States of America

First Edition, 2023

This book is dedicated to
the most extraordinary person I will ever know,
my beautiful Mother,
**Ana M. Young.**
The extraordinary surpasses the ordinary
in all life's stages, at all moments in time.
The most extraordinary are not paralyzed by fear,
but driven by it.
They refuse to accept the standard and
see the potential in everything,
all while relishing in the beauty of everyday life.

She is extraordinary,
the most extraordinary of all.

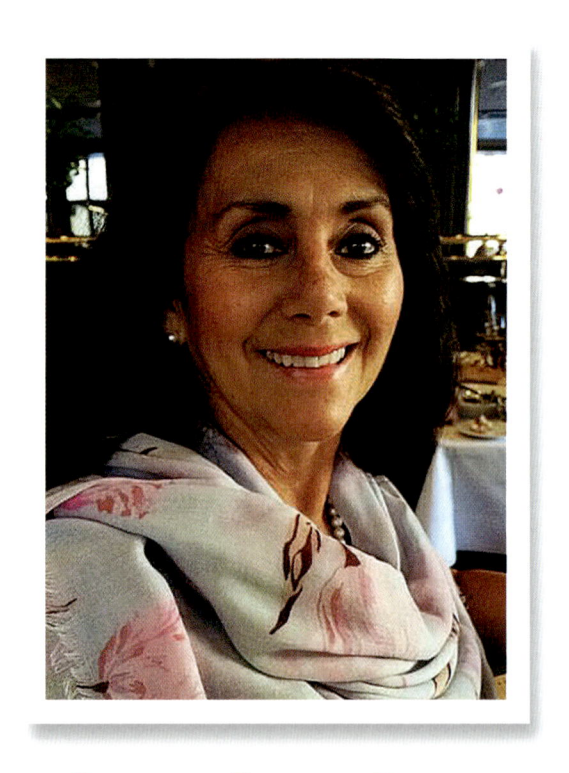

*Ana M. Young*

# Contents

| | | |
|---|---|---|
| Preface | | vii |
| Chapter 1 | Lost and Found | 1 |
| Chapter 2 | Manager Speak | 5 |
| Chapter 3 | No Babysitters Allowed | 17 |
| Chapter 4 | Marvelous Mom | 35 |
| Chapter 5 | The Beauty is in the Details | 51 |
| Chapter 6 | No Ordinary Day | 63 |
| Chapter 7 | A Life to Stomach | 83 |
| Chapter 8 | My Queen | 95 |
| Chapter 9 | Gold Leaf | 113 |
| Chapter 10 | Letters of Life | 127 |
| Chapter 11 | The Miracle | 155 |
| Portfolio | | 160 |
| Afterword | | 179 |

*Catherine Anne Young*

# Preface

My name is Catherine Anne Young, and I am a twenty-eight-year-old debut author. I was born and raised in Tampa, Florida by two of the most loving and supportive parents, William Joseph Young and Ana Margarita Young. Both of my parents were born in Guatemala City, Guatemala, which granted my sister, Margaret Anne, and I exposure to another world rich in culture, and brimming with family and food. With the exception of the "tickle fights" phase, my sister is my forever-best friend—growing up with her and our extended family members in Guatemala made our lives that much more wondrous.

After Tampa, I moved to South Bend, Indiana where I quickly became familiar with terms such as "polar vortex" and "lake effect" at the University of Notre Dame. Despite this character-building experience for the unknowing Floridian, I managed to graduate with a degree in Business and Italian and made lifelong friends. I studied abroad in Paris, London, and Rome, and learned the art of the Natural Light shotgun at football games. I currently reside in Cincinnati, Ohio, where I work in sales as an account manager for General Mills, and where I do in fact consume Cinnamon Toast Crunch regularly.

As for my first book, the only credentials that could potentially pass for writing experience include creating a poem in the tenth grade that was published in my high school magazine, correcting friends' grammar on a frequent occurrence, and somehow crafting a successful college admissions essay about my passion for chocolate chip cookies. However, what I lack in expertise, I make up for in gumption to spread my mother's inspirational story to any and all willing to read.

When Ana Young is your mother, your life unravels in a way unparalleled to most. The experiences, perspective, countenance, and faith you foster unleash a series of events some can only concoct in a dream.

My beautiful mother inspired me from the very beginning of my life. Everything I ever did was in direct response to her example. From eating blue cheese at age three, to wanting to shop at Talbot's at age eight, I duplicated her every move in the hopes I too would grow up to be as magnificent as she was. This enchantment with my mother was not founded upon blind childish following, but rather due to how she carried herself from the onset of my memory.

This love for her poured out of me in the form of this book, just as naturally as a forbidden secret escapes from the mouth of an eager child. But unlike a forbidden secret, my incredible mother's journey should not be kept quiet. So, here's hoping this book exceeds my tenth-grade teacher's expectations, my grammatically inept friends' punctuation, and the captivating narrative of the Publix chocolate chip cookie.

I want to thank everyone who supported me in compiling this testament to my mother's magnificence. These individuals include my father, William Joseph Young, and sister, Margaret Anne Young, as well as other close family and friends. I also want to thank my Keurig machine, for all the late-night caffeine doses. I truly could not have written this book without the sweet nectar of your caffeinated creations.

Before I begin, it must also be noted that I love my father beyond belief. He is my rock and I do not know where I would be without him. His unwavering support and introspectiveness have helped shape me into becoming the person I am today. I also know my sense of humor would not significantly lean into "dad jokes" territory, a crucial part of my persona some would say, if it were not for "mon père."

My fascination with my mother does not lessen my love or appreciation for my father. On the contrary, it strengthened as a result. My father was completely entranced with my mother. He understands the enchantment I have always had for My Queen because he too loved and cared for her in an awe-inspiring way. He taught me what it is I should look for in a partner of life, someone whose patience and love transcend even the hardest of obstacles. Thus, our mutual fascination for all things Ana Young made us closer. He was never plagued by jealousy or saddened by the shadow of her attention, all because he understood the miracle that is my beautiful mom.

This is a story about a woman with cancer. However, it is not your typical cancer story, by any means. It's not going to start with a diagnosis, continue with a courageous battle, and end with either a victory or a loss. This is the compilation of fragments of time, moments that underscore the power of human existence, highlight the potency of possibility, and capture the beauty of the love of a mother. This is the story of a spectacular human with a resilience so impressive it inspired this very book. It is the story of a fearless individual, unscathed by the word "no" and unsusceptible to the comfort of complacency. This is the powerful narrative of a human so far beyond the normalcy of mortal beings that every beautiful sunset and every majestic sunrise falls short of capturing her magnificence. Yes, this is a tale about a woman with cancer, a woman who you would have never suspected possessed such a demoralizing disease. The way she lived. The courage she showed. The love and faith that ultimately extended her earth-bound life. That is what this book is about. That is what I hope to give to you: perspective, hope, and perhaps a smile or two.

This is the story of my beautiful mother, my inspiration for all, my favorite person in the whole world. This is a book about Ana M. Young, My Queen, and how she never let anything get in the way of living the most extraordinary life.

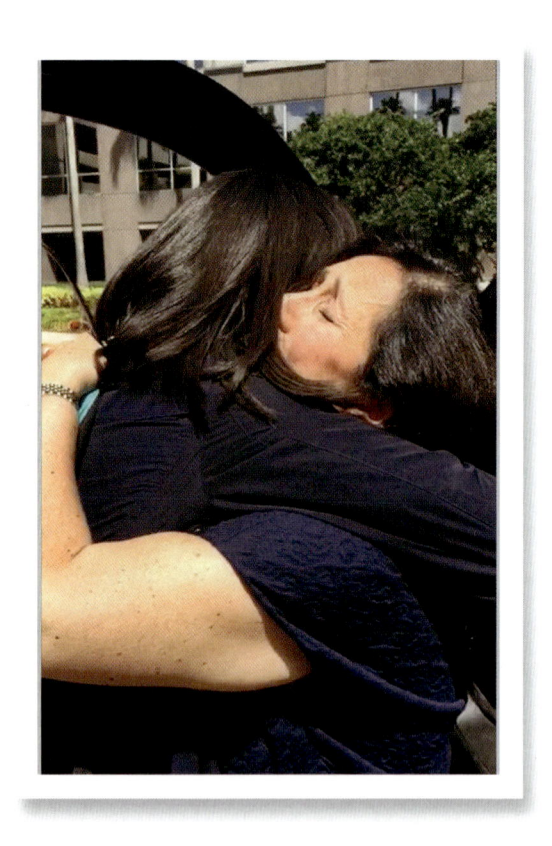

*My mother and I embracing when I surprised her for Easter in 2017.*

CHAPTER ONE

# Lost & Found

*Read and pray, every day.*

MAY 8, 2000

When Ana Young is your mother, your first instinct when lost in New York City is to cry out, "Mommy!!!"

I begin to pace back and forth from one end of the block to the other, praying to God my beautiful mother's face would appear.

"Mommy! Mommy! Mommy!!!" I started shouting, now at a higher pitch with growing severity.

The thought of getting separated from the most beautiful woman in the world was the underlying reason for the panic that set in. And then, a light emerged from "New York's Finest" pizzeria… an angelic silhouette quickly approached me, blurred by the tears of my panic. In an instant, my sweet mother's embrace stifled the crisis, and I was reunited once again with God's greatest gift: an embrace by Ana M. Young. Oh, how happy I was to be home!

I was seven years old.

You can only imagine the trauma of the first day of school in Tampa when I was four.

"How on Earth am I to survive the trials of Ms. Hildebrandt's kindergarten class without My Queen? Seven whole hours? I demand to know who came up with this ungodly concept of separation!" My four-year-old self pondered as I hugged my mother's leg harder to avoid my scholastic obligations.

"It's time to go inside," the sweet angel said to me as I nearly cut blood circulation from her leg.

And so, with severe hesitation, I let go and prayed for a miracle as I waved goodbye to my best friend.

I wish I could say God answered my prayer, and that kindergarten was the best year of my life. On the contrary, I sat on the bench during recess every day for three weeks crying about missing My Mommy. It was as if I had been incessantly chopping onions for weeks on end every day at exactly 10 a.m. Not only is it an incredibly weird morning activity, but also a physiological detriment to one's tear ducts. And yet, I couldn't help it. I was the chopped-onion girl with a strong semblance to a melancholy Dora the Explorer.

Thankfully, I had a friend, Alex Viso, who would join me on said bench to try and console me during this very trying time. But not even Alex Viso could stop my sadness. I was convinced I was unsalvageable.

Eventually, the hugs goodbye became less difficult and the after-school reunions grew into such joyous occasions that I finally acclimated to my new routine. I began loving school. I learned how wonderful it felt to expand upon curiosity, and how satisfying it was to answer a question correctly.

I remember looking at myself in front of the mirror of the living room armoire, saying, "I'm always going to do my best. I don't know why people don't just try their hardest. Why not do your best always? That's what I'm going to do."

Looking back upon this moment in time, there is only one possible explanation for why a young, five-year-old girl would experience such a revelation: Ana Young. Since the very beginning, my mother's example sparked this fire within me. Her story of dedication, intellectual cultivation, and resilience allowed me to see firsthand what hard work can do, how dreams and challenges push you to go further, and how to overcome your own "chopped onion" phases altogether.

This is the incredible story of Ana M. Young, my beautiful mother, and the miracle that was her life.

*Ana giving her Valedictorian speech during her graduation from Colegio Gibbs in 1973.*

CHAPTER TWO

# Manager Speak

*Life is about learning as much as you can, and then turning that knowledge into action.*

**FEBRUARY 2, 2019**

When Ana Young is your mother, you frequently hear the following request, "Can I speak with your manager?" My beautiful mother said this sweetly, yet sternly to the hostess at the restaurant.

After having already been seated at a less than agreeable table, my mother spoke the words that were both feared and praised by many. Feared mostly by the employees and managers themselves due to my gregarious mother's formidable appeal and praised by her family members for whom the complaint would most often benefit. However, no matter the request, if Ana Young spoke these words, it was inevitable: game, set, match. The deal was done.

My beautiful mother, don't get me wrong, was the sweetest, most well-intentioned human to walk the earth. But if you ever got in her way, crossed her–or her daughters–you would find yourself giving in to her demands faster than you can say, "Where is the nearest exit?" She was an absolute angel, but she was also a go-getter, firm in her beliefs and relentless until she achieved her goals. I used to compare her to a doll: a precious petite piece of porcelain perfection. However, if the doll were to get angry and come to life, you lose all notions of reality and become crippled with fear until fulfilling the conscious figurine's demands.

Through my lovable mother's persistence and personable demeanor, she accomplished incredible feats. Out of fear of rejection, complacency, or simple lack of will, many people settle for the cards they've been dealt and fail to go that extra mile.

Ana Young lacked the word *settle* in her vocabulary. She owned permanent real estate in the *extra mile*.

She said and went beyond what the normal person would consider *standard*, achieving tasks both large and small. Gift of the gab? Maybe, but the real reason I believe for her success in persuasion stems from her willingness to try.

In certain uncomfortable situations—and believe me there were these moments—my mother would always say, "Worst thing that can happen is they say no!" At the time, I thought to myself the worst thing would also include the subsequent walk of shame from the coveted table by the fish tank to our original table in the back by the bathrooms. But Ana never focused on this outcome. She saw beyond what most see as the "here and now." She focused her attention on the power of possibility. Because why not more?

It was this line of thinking that led her in 2004 to meet and kiss the hand of Pope John Paul II, now recognized a saint by the Catholic Church. It was the contributing factor as to how she had a picture taken with President George and Laura Bush, worthy of our family's Christmas card, despite the absence of my father and me in the photograph. It is also the reason why my family has had more pleasant culinary experiences at dining institutions. She had initiative and never settled. And never, ever gave up.

Her favorite movie of all time was *The Sound of Music*, in large part because of the song, "Climb Every Mountain." Just as the von Trapps had to escape the grips of the Nazi regime, my mother understood that we all have mountains of our own we must climb. Thus, whenever a "mountain" took form in her life, her sense of self fueled her to climb higher.

Lines of immigration were no exception. In Miami, on occasion, the way to get back into the United States after a family trip to Guatemala looked like what I envision Ellis Island to look like after the start of the First World War: complete chaos and a never-ending line. Most people would just get in line and hope to God they wouldn't miss their connecting flight. But not my mother. She always made it a point to speak with an immigration officer to allow our family through a different, faster line, usually using the excuse that my father was in the military.

And sure enough, as soon as they caught a glimpse of my mother's shimmering smile and docile eyes, we were escorted to the diplomat section where only eight people stood rather than eighteen hundred.

Some may think "complicated" would describe this type of behavior, but I would have to lean more towards "majestically advanced."

A Hispanic Mary Poppins, if you will.

Her successes also stemmed from her confidence. She knew, from the start, the value of her voice, and the pertinence of her presence. For example, my father one day extended her a statement of praise, claiming she was "one in a million." My mother, however, was offended by the statement, claiming "one in a million" was far too common.

Other compliments highlighted this confidence.

"I love your hair, it is absolutely stunning," expressed an unknown lady at the mall.

Now usually one would respond with some form of pleasantry, such as "thank you" or "shucks, you shouldn't have."

But remember, my mother was not from this world.

She would respond with, "I know, right?" completely agreeing with the comment extended.

This confidence allowed her to break down barriers and open doors for herself and for her family. It's also the reason why she loved photos. She truly was a beautiful lady with magnificent physical attributes. She had thick, dark brown hair, large, yet soft brown eyes, with eyelids big enough for a painter's canvas. Her nose perked up slightly, with a curvature seemingly flattened by God himself. Her chin held a small dent, a similarity she shared with her father. Her cheeks soft and rosy, with a bone structure that would make any celebrity envious. Her mouth refined and smile golden, with pearly whites that never needed any kind of alteration. She had a perfect face. And to top it all off, her adorable 5'2" stature made her all the more lovely. She was stunning, and I for the longest time thought I had a real-life Barbie Doll as a mother.

It was this alluring physique that captivated the one and only Joe DiMaggio when my father and mother saw him at National Airport in Washington DC in 1990. Rather than adhering to his alleged misanthropic behavior when approached by fans, my father says Mr. DiMaggio's eyes lit up when he saw my mother, just as if he had just seen Marilyn Monroe for the first time. He was warm and asked my parents for forgiveness for seeming distracted since his suitcase appeared to have been stolen by a fan. After a quick shake, they separated, with my dad bewildered at the first *Forrest Gump* moment he experienced due to my mother's presence.

"I am absolutely certain, had I walked up to Joe DiMaggio by myself, he would have brushed me aside. But because I was with Mom (a beautiful lady—and he appreciated beautiful women), he welcomed us with open arms, and allowed me a glimpse of what it was like to be next to a national hero," my father recounts.

Aside from my mother's physical beauty, her true appeal stemmed from the depth of her soul and the great power of her brain.

Growing up, my mother was no different. As the eldest of four siblings, Olga María Solares de Bosch, José Rafael Solares, and Juan Alfonso Solares, my mother learned the importance of leadership and responsibility at a very young age. So much was she programmed to take the reins of command, that when my grandparents would travel abroad, my punctilious mother was left in charge of her brothers, sister, and household staff. Her proclivity in the art of responsibility surfaced, leaving everyone allegedly "starved" during her parents' absence, due to her strict adherence to my grandparents' food rationing.

"Can we have more rice?" my uncle asked his stringent caretaker, but to no avail.

"No," she replied matter-of-factly, as though living through the Great Bengal famine of 1943. "Mother and Father have left me with a limited portion of supplies, so it is my job to ensure we have enough until they return."

Although seemingly draconian, her sense of responsibility complemented the tremendous amount of care she extended her loved ones, knowing that each grain of rice had to be accounted for to ensure proper nourishment for her growing siblings.

Another example of her natural-born leadership derives from the talent shows my mother would orchestrate in which her siblings and cousins performed for the elders. As the director, choreographer, ticket collector, and administrator, Ana Young sure knew how to put on a show, making all other child-cast productions laden with lemonade stand naivety.

And that was just on weekends.

In elementary school, my mother even recounts her leadership in the school bus. Due to her maturity and trustworthiness, the school principal granted my mother the responsibility of ensuring all fellow children behaved during the daily transport. Her priority? A smooth ride for all who rode. The outcome? A further heightening of a seven-year-old's journey towards self-actualization.

This focus in life, elevated by the pairing of her intrinsic curiosity for the cultivation of the mind and the example of her father, guided her academic pursuits as she progressed further into adulthood.

My mother did her best in all levels of schooling. Whether it was reciting a poem for English class, or completing a final exam, she placed her best efforts in all she did, no matter how small a task. Without the awareness of the competitive landscape, her strict adherence to excellence led her to achieving the coveted title of Valedictorian in high school. Turns out, there were several females fending for the title in her all-girl high school, but my mother, unaware of their jealousy and ambition, simply performed as usual, putting her powerful brain to work and ultimately secured the victory.

    In addition, she was so far beyond her peer set, that her principal decided to pull her out of high school early since she was fully prepared for the following phase: Marymount College in the United States. A Catholic college for women at the time (now a coed university) in Arlington, Virginia, my mother spoke dearly about the several adventures she experienced at Marymount: how she and her friends used to go to Georgetown to meet local gentlemen, use dining hall trays to sled down snowy hills in the wintertime, how she lost an orange bed sheet in the middle of winter, later found due to the stark contrast of the bleak white snow, how she befriended the most wonderful roommate Jeannie Gross from New Jersey, singing in the "Glebe" Club (clever use of the college's street: North Glebe Road), having a boyfriend named Bill (coincidentally also the name of my father) who was the neighbor of Senator John Glenn, and loving every minute she spent feeding her brain through scholastic stimulation.

    Despite my mother's enriching experiences and academic scholarship, my grandparents decided to bring My Queen back home to where she was born and raised, Guatemala City, Guatemala. Located in Central America, where it is bounded by Mexico, Belize, Honduras, and El Salvador, Guatemala is a country rich in culture and tradition. As a predominantly Christian land, faith and family are the most important facets of a person's life, seen through the kind-hearted locals and lack of career-first mentalities characteristic of the United States. As a developing country, numerous opportunities exist for Guatemala, explaining the frequent mission trips that take place to help impoverished areas. However, what it lacks in infrastructure it makes up for in charm with over half of the population indigenous to the Mayan civilization. These individuals usually sport multi-colored hand-woven tunics and are famous for crafting impressive textiles and delicious cuisine. Perhaps the inhabitants are a jovial group due to the year-round idyllic weather, earning itself the nickname, "The Land of Eternal Spring." The landscape is also quite awe-inspiring, with over twenty volcanoes, impressive mountains, ancient ruins, and unique flora and fauna permeating the country.

    Despite all of Guatemala's amazing attributes, my mother was not ready to come home. Her parents however had their reasons. First involved the social construct of prioritizing a male's education over that of a female. My grandparents believed my mother had completed an appropriate amount of time cultivating her mind, claiming it was her brothers' and sister's turn to delve into the world of higher education. A land dominated by the beliefs of male governance and female subservience. Guatemala at that time was certainly a challenging environment for ambitious young women, such as my mother. Although it may sound harsh and unjust to have stripped something so valuable, like education, from such a promising student, my grandparents were merely following the mentality of the era. In reality, they were always very proud of their dear Ana Margarita, acknowledging fully how blessed they were to have such an amazing daughter who excelled in all she did.

    My mother was taken out of college also because my grandparents did not want my mother marrying an American since it meant she would most likely stay in the United States. Little did they know their Anita would end up marrying my father, a U.S. Air Force officer who led her to the United States as a permanent resident.

    A brief pause to note something about my father. As a fervent admirer of the United States, Ana was always very proud of being married to a military officer. She constantly mentioned how my father serving in the military introduced her to other worlds, including when he was stationed at the Pentagon in Washington D.C., and at MacDill Air Force Base in Tampa, Florida. It was a surreal experience for her, but also became the norm. There she was buying everyday items like groceries, school supplies, and clothing on one of the most important military bases in the world. My father lovingly recounts how my mother would interrupt high-intensity, time-sensitive meetings just to ask him to buy milk and eggs on his way home. This helped my father put things back into perspective and aided him in coping with the stressful nature of a Lieutenant Colonel's responsibilities. Of course, there were also times of great stress for my family, such as when he was deployed to the Middle East in support of Operation Enduring Freedom in 2003, 2004, and 2005. Thankfully, my father returned home every time, claiming those moments abroad were some of the most rewarding experiences he's ever had.

Beyond his travel, my father's job was always a mystery.

Whenever I used to ask my dad what he actually did for work, the most common answer I'd receive was, "Vaporizing personnel that mean to harm the United States."

To cause trepidation amongst my boyfriends, however, my father shortened his response to: "I vaporize people for a living."

To this day, I'm still not sure about the validity of such a claim, in part because I never could partake in "take your daughter to work day." What I do know is whatever my father's daily tasks entailed, it was always for the good of the nation, fostering my family's undying love of country.

When my mother married my father on July 27, 1991, her principal and lifelong friend, María Marta de Klanderud told him, *"Te llevas lo mejor de Guatemala."* (Translation: You are taking the best of Guatemala).

She was not wrong in the slightest. My mother was one of the most beloved women in the entire country. She was the closest thing Guatemala had to royalty.

Now back to my mother in Marymount. And so, with a heavy heart, Ana left her collegiate haven with an associate degree in business and a heavy heart.

However, not even the era's collective obstacles could stop the yearning for greatness so characteristic of Ana Young. Despite the time's societal barriers, my mother received her degree as a translator in Guatemala, and she worked more jobs than most people do today. My brilliant mother worked at twelve different locations. That's right, twelve. One for each day of Christmas, one for each Krispy Kreme donut in a classic dozen. A few of these professional corporations include: IDB (International Development Bank), Bank of Chicago, The World Bank, and Lancasco, S.A. She even aided in the work of bringing the Domino's Pizza franchise to Guatemala.

    My mother's talents extended beyond intellectual prowess and occupational triumph. She also had an incredible eye for design and architectural creation. Even beyond these twelve work experiences, my mother helped construct my grandparents' beautiful summer home in Guatemala's old capital, Antigua. A land lost in time, this Spanish colonial-style city is home to cobblestone roads, antiquated churches and ruins, horse-drawn carriages, impressive volcanoes, and mountains guarding the city. It has a large population of individuals of Mayan decent. It was my darling mother's favorite place to frequent, with the house as her Shangri-La. She helped her parents make decisions on what type of windows to use, doors to install, and stone to pave what is now La Plaza Ana, a serene walkway from the main outdoor patio to the pool, lined with floral accents and a lemon tree. My mother used to recount meetings with Amerigo, the engineer and architect that helped construct the magnificent home, featured once in the magazine *Estilos & Casas* for its brilliance. My grandparents even decided to add a chapel there, where my sister and I were both baptized, and held our First Communion. It was also the venue for my parents' wedding reception, as well as numerous birthday celebrations. That house means everything to me because it meant the world to my mother. It was one of her proudest accomplishments.

    "You are wise beyond your years," my grandfather would often say to My Queen.

    In fact, I would so often hear this phrase, that when tasked with forming a sentence with the word *wise* in Mrs. Arthurs's first grade spelling class, I used the decree, "My mother is very wise."

And she was. In addition to everything mentioned, she was also a scholar of the arts. Her love and appreciation of classical music started as a little girl in my grandfather's study. "When the piano started playing in Beethoven's Piano Concerto, No. 5, 'The Emperor,' I just fell in love with classical music," my mother shared, pinpointing the exact moment when the tale as old as time commenced.

My mother was very similar to my grandfather. They shared complementary values and perspectives on life, especially in their fascination with orchestral chamber music. After listening to a piece of music, they both had this incredible ability to discern the name of a composition and determine its composer. I remember yearning for this talent since I was a little girl, but even after all these years, I still rely on technology to ascertain the artist.

The only thing I remember my grandfather and mother disagreed on was their take on having a favorite composer. For example, when my grandfather was asked which composer was his favorite, he always used to say, "How do you expect me to choose between a roast chicken and a piece of strawberry cake?"

On the other hand, my mother, without hesitation, always singled out George Frideric Handel as her predilection due to the undeniable majesty in each of his pieces. This admiration drove our family to the Tampa Oratorio Singer's annual performance of Handel's "Messiah" every year during Christmastime.

At my mother's suggestion, one year in elementary school, I invited my best friend in the third grade to join in on the musical experience. Poor Victoria Litschgi was so bored throughout the two-hour-long orchestral performance that I was concerned I had jeopardized our friendship.

Quite overtaken by the majesty of Handel's *Messiah*, my mother even tried to bring the classical music concert to our high school, The

Academy of the Holy Names of Jesus and Mary. After countless meetings with our school's President, and the Oratorio Singer's distinguished director Nancy Callahan, my mother put in her best effort to bring awareness of such powerful music to those around her. Despite such attempts, the school deemed the performance far beyond the caliber and comprehension of the average student. They used the excuse that most students would fail to appreciate the choral majesty, and thus, the time and effort would be better spent elsewhere. Although the results were not favorable, it further highlights the intrinsic noblesse so characteristic of My Queen. Ana Young was on a level far beyond that of the common man. She was above Aaron Copland's *Fanfare*, and more in line with Handel's coronation anthems.

With her impressive resumé and an even more astounding performance while watching *Jeopardy*, Ana Young's successes are too vast to fathom. However, despite all her accolades and points of recognition, Ana would say her greatest success came from the most important job she held, her thirteenth position if you will: motherhood.

*My mother, sister, father, and I
with our grandparents in their home in
Guatemala City, Guatemala.*

CHAPTER THREE

# No Babysitters Allowed

*Knowledge is power.*

**OCTOBER 23, 1998**

When Ana Young is your mother, the word *babysitter* did not enter your vocabulary until friends from school introduced the concept. For all you knew, it meant a trained professional skilled in the art of being seated atop America's youth.

My mother did not believe in babysitters. Wherever my parents went, there we were. From having cocktail hour with friends of my grandparents, to dinners in fancy restaurants in which we were always the youngest to partake, Margaret Anne, my elder sister, and I grew up adapting to all sorts of environments. As time went by and we grew older, our cousins always asked us why we never contested the compulsory adult activities. But we knew we were being led by the great Ana Young, and following her usually led to something extraordinary.

There had to be a greater reason why we were destined to follow suit. And there was. Because our mother didn't believe in babysitters, we were exposed to the exchange of ideas of some of the greatest minds of our time. We learned the importance of respecting one's elders, the power of conversation, as well as the necessity of patience and adaptability.

By attending such receptions and gatherings, Margaret Anne and I also learned how to perform in front of crowds. You must be wondering how on earth would attending a cocktail hour warrant some sort of display of talent? I'll explain. You see, because my parents were so proud of the two little girls they were raising, they would want to show off our abilities, which (in theory) boosted our confidence.

    The first childhood performance I remember involved singing "The Button Factory" song in which one took on the persona of Fred, a confused factory worker who for some reason, was never busy, and regardless of previous misgivings, would continue to sing and push buttons for the extension of different body parts. Once this song lost its *cuteness* factor and approached *worrisome* territory, our next major number was singing the surprise musical ending of the classic film *Shrek*. There was no particular reason why this song was chosen, other than the captivating performance of a dancing green ogre, so characteristic of any swamp-obsessed child of age six. And yes, choreography was involved. Another crowd favorite was the "Gobble, Gobble" song, a Thanksgiving ballad about a weight-conscious turkey who was keenly aware of the repercussions of having a corpulent composition around the holidays. This number became so popular, that our extended family members had the pleasure of enjoying it year-round.

    Once my sister grew older, however, and her level of embarrassment became more unpredictable, she began to learn the art of saying "no" to such requests. I think she drew the line after my mother asked her to sing the *Our Father* in Latin in front of a few family friends. That was the day I became a solo artist.

    I, on the other hand, had no trouble continuing with the displays of talent, due to the subsequent smiles from my parents' faces. Knowing full-well everything I have is a result of their generosity and wonderful parenting, I grew up thriving from their satisfaction and pride in my triumphs with tasks, large and small. One classic Catherine performance was the dance routine, "The Movement of the Waves," in which I'd reenact the motion of water as it reached the shore. In my mind I was creating a complex interpretative dance, demonstrative of water's fluidity and grandeur. In reality, I was simply jolting my head back after one or two movements of a violent Hula dance. However unusual though, the crowd, i.e., my parents and grandparents, would always go crazy for it. Given its popularity, one day, my uncle, Tío Joey, decided to join the routine. I will never forget the laughter and applause that ensued once he became part of the number. Together, we were unstoppable.

Another popular demonstration of "talent" was the act in which I took on the character of an older Greek immigrant in search of the American dream, inspired of course by the film *My Big Fat Greek Wedding*.

"I come to America with eight dollars in my pocket," I would start, with a thick Grecian accent and my grandmother's shawl draped over my head to help with the illusion.

As the story progressed, and I knew I had my audience captivated, I began to discern common words of Greek origin, completely without regard to the veracity of my conjectures.

"Did you know trampoline comes from the Greek word *trampoli*, which means leg? What do you use on a trampoline to jump? A leg. Trampoline, leg, there you go!"

I know this skit is nowhere near the same level of funny as SNL, probably not even in the same comedic neighborhood as knock-knock jokes, but there was something about it that had my entire family cracking up.

Aside from the adrenaline rush from recounting my "immigrant days," I would also give into my parents' wishes at an older age due to everything I put them through during my terrible twos. If one is the loneliest number, two most definitely is the angriest. There is one moment in time that captured the essence of my irritable two-year-old self. Let me rephrase: my irritable-with-everything-except-Mom self.

In our pre-school, Hyde Park Day School, there was a yearly ceremony in which Mr. Q and Mrs. U get married to convey the concept that in the English language, the letters Q and U are always together. It came as no surprise that my sister was chosen as Mrs. U, and thus, my mother orchestrated an event as though Margaret Anne was actually taking part in toddler matrimony. Despite having only experienced four years of life, the blooming bride wore a beautiful, hand-made wedding gown all the way from Spain, along with a French lace veil that made her resemble the byproduct of a toymaker's craftsmanship. There was also a three-tiered cake, exquisitely decorated and extravagantly large, enough to feed her class three times over. The stark contrast with the groom's cake, a generic Thomas the Tank Engine cake clearly purchased that morning at a local Publix, was almost embarrassing. White rose petals lined the small benches down the aisle, and Margaret Anne's "groom" stood reluctantly at the front, evidently fighting the urge to use the bathroom. It truly was the fake wedding of the century.

On the day of the ceremony, my parents decided to focus some time and attention on their unbetrothed, grammatically irrelevant child.

"What do you want for Christmas?" asked the mother of the alphabet bride.

"I want a Barbie, with calzoneta, and eewings," I responded in English, Spanish, and a language resembling English but inadvertently omitting the letter **r**.

My dad, wanting to shake things up a bit, probed further, "You don't want a baseball bat?"

Trouble began to brew.

"Noooooo," I respond in a deeper, more enraged voice, frustrated that somehow my previous statement had failed to register, "I want a Barbie with calzoneta and eewings!"

My dad, finding humor in the situation, continued, "How about a baseball glove?"

I wish I could fully explain what happened next, but I think the most accurate description would entail replaying a scene from *The Exorcist*.

"NOOOO, I want a Barbie with calzoneta and eewings!!!" This

time completely beside myself, and on the verge of unleashing the Niagara Falls of tears.

My beautiful mother understood the gravity of the situation, and quickly deployed a tactic to restore the peace, "My Catarini, how does the song in *Anastasia* go again?"

Upon hearing my sweet angel's voice, I was immediately calmed, and proceeded to sing, "Once Upon a December" as requested.

Ana Young had saved the day yet again, and I gave the performance of a lifetime.

Terrible twos aside, in addition to building character, this practice of performing in front of crowds is one of the reasons why Margaret Anne and I have no trouble speaking in front of large groups of people. It's also the reason why I've always appreciated musicals.

Beyond song and dance, the performances extended to our educational tenure. I'm not talking about the famous Young sister performances at our school talent show. Rather, I'm alluding to the inordinate number of times my sister and I carried out duties during our all-school Masses. Wanting us to always be the best and knowing our far-reaching capabilities, our beautiful mother would call Sister Mary Patricia Plum, the orchestrator of our school's liturgical celebrations, and ask for us to be tasked with reading or carrying the gifts during Mass. This was not my favorite activity, as it was a daunting experience to have 400-plus eyes on you as you prayed to God more fervently than you did during any spiritual assembly.

"Oh, please God, help me to not trip or fall," I repeated over and over as my hand trembled for fear of dropping the Eucharist and preventing our entire school from participating in Most Holy Communion.

Normally my sister was right next to me. As the eldest, she naturally held the burden of carrying the heavier of the two objects, the chalice of wine, more susceptible to spillage with irregular movements. God bless her.

The worst part about this was the fact that I could not catch a break, even on my birthday. Now it is important to mention how much I love my birthday. It is an absolute sacred day during which I enjoy celebrating with only my favorite things. Having been born on the Feast Day of the Immaculate Conception, celebrated on December 8, a Holy Day of Obligation in the Catholic faith, a day when Catholics are obliged to go to Mass, my mother would sign me up for some variation of sacramental duties. The last thing I wanted to do that day was go through the panic of potentially slipping on my sister's spilled wine.

"My Mommy, please, not this year. I just want to enjoy my birthday!" I pleaded.

"*No Cath, es algo bueno! Es un lujo!* (Translation: No Cath, it's something good! It's an honor!" She countered, with her docile eyes that convinced me faster than you can say "Body of Christ."

It was the same thing every year.

And yet after the brief stint of anxiety preceding Mass, every time we carried out these duties, we were met with much praise and gratitude by all who partook. And thus, the satisfaction of completing our Catholic tasks began to overshadow the negative sentiments, with each subsequent occurrence becoming easier and easier to execute. Reading the Prayers of Intercessions? Sure! Taking up the gifts to the altar? No problem! We became experts in dealing with large crowds, a core competency that we carry forward to this very day.

Another example of the incredible foresight and wisdom of Mom was the act of talking over the phone. Every time someone from Guatemala called our house, my mother, without warning or request from the person calling, would hand over the phone to me and my sister.

"*Aquí está Cath que la quiere saludar* (Translation: Here is Cath, she wants to say hi)," my mother would say, quickly letting go of the phone as if it were sweltering hot.

I, in fact, did not want to say hi. I wanted to keep my hand submerged in the Cheetos bag where it belonged. And yet, I found myself diving into a ten-minute conversation with my uncle, who I can assure you also let out a discernible sigh once my mother invited a third party to their call.

She would even do this to my grandmother, who would reluctantly answer after my mother quickly passed the phone as though participating in hot potato.

"*No mijita, no quiero hablar con nadie* (Translation: No, my daughter, I don't want to talk with anyone)," Abuela would complain, as my mother's glaring stare and imperceptible mouthing of words informed my grandmother that she had no choice in the matter, and was thus handed the phone.

This constant exposure to landline communication also extended to family members' birthdays. Birthday salutations were stressful because at a young age, it was tough to be a conversationalist when your main priorities involved spending time with Mom, eating, and Barbie dolls with eewings. Consequently, I really didn't have much to talk about with my slightly older male cousins. As the youngest, however, I was always the last person to speak, with most topics already exhausted by my mother, father, and sister. Thus, after much sweat and strife, I learned the art of recycling questions. My sister usually laughed at me as I struggled through the call because I clearly had nothing else to ask besides what was already thrown out there. These included, "What are you doing to celebrate? What did you get for presents? Do you feel older?" Looking back upon these agonizing minutes of forced exchanges, I now realize the genius behind it all. Because of these experiences, I learned not only the invaluable skill of talking over the phone, but also when to stop eating Cheetos.

No babysitters also led to the great adventures spent with the magnificent humans who raised my miraculous mother. The only plausible explanation for the existence of a Hispanic Mary Poppins, is for said "Mary" to have grown up in a loving household, raised by superior individuals. Don Rafael Felipe Solares Riépele and Olga Concepción

Camacho de Solares fostered a household haven in which my mother fondly recounts the happiest of childhoods. Despite living within their means, my grandfather worked ceaselessly as a businessman tending to the pharmaceutical company he pioneered. He was determined to provide a better tomorrow for his family while Abuela provided the motherly affection My Queen and her three siblings needed growing up.

This foundation, built on love and hard work, with which my mother commenced her life, propelled her for an existence of love, respect, and admiration for her parents. And so, even in adulthood, my mother always made it a point to include the two most influential people in her life in ours.

This need to involve my grandparents in everything led to wondrous memories. We were the unbeatable sextet that took on Las Vegas, Disney, the West, New York, and all other sorts of lands and landscapes. With my mother's enthusiastic agenda, my father's sarcasm, my grandfather's knowledge, and grandmother's hugs, the times spent together were nothing short of extraordinary.

To add to the fun of our traveling adventures, in addition to serving as a self-preservation tactic against my sister's pranks and father's teasing, I implemented a contest we used to do in kindergarten: The Star Chart. The premise was simple: cater to my needs through acts of service and kindness, and you'd receive a star. The individual with the greatest number of stars at the end of the vacation would be crowned the victor and receive a certificate and prize. The certificate usually manifested itself on a hotel napkin, and the prize directly correlated with the phrase, *one man's trash is another's treasure* (i.e., the prize was literal trash I crafted from the limited resources available to a young lady of six). Usually, my mother would win by a landslide. However, to motivate all participants, my grandfather, grandmother, and even Tío Joey took the *W* from time to time. As for my sister and father, to this day they have never won a Star Chart contest.

So extraordinary was the time spent with my grandparents, that even beyond the scope of travel, when los Abuelos came to Tampa, it was an all-consuming happiness, synonymous to the feeling of going to Disney World. Once the overwhelming aroma of Pledge, Windex, and carpet cleaner filled our house, my sister and I knew times of merriment were imminent.

As a family of many traditions, one of them was that every time they visited, we would have dinner on the first night at The Colonnade, an iconic restaurant on Bayshore Boulevard in Tampa. This establishment, although seemingly catered to an elderly clientele, became one of my favorite restaurants because it meant we were all together again, amidst a sea of sweater vests.

One of the usual activities when the "greatest package deal" made their way to Florida involved going to the mall. Although women of great depth, my mother and grandmother loved to shop and take part in the materialistic commercialism characteristic of the United States. As a man of much patience and as a strong admirer of the female mystique, my grandfather without complaint, would accompany his wife on her spending trips. It became a routine for him to enter a shop, ask the clerk where one could find a chair, and sit in said chair for hours until the shopping ended. Knowing the joy it brought his wife and daughter, sometimes my grandfather would discover sales in the daily newspaper and present his findings as though in support of strengthening the U.S. economy.

One of these sales was that of Lord & Taylor during its liquidation period in 2004. One Monday morning during summer vacation, my beautiful mother wakes me up and tells me what was planned for the day.

"We are going to go shopping at Lord & Taylor because everything is 50% off," she stated, wearing her perfect hair and beautiful smile.

And so, I quickly got ready, and accompanied my family on our capitalistic journey. After a long day of perusing the store's products, we finally returned to the refuge of Seagate Drive (street name of my childhood home).

The next morning, I woke up to a similar awakening, "Good morning, my Catarini. We are going back to Lord & Taylor because el Abuelo says everything is now 60% off!"

Despite sitting all day in the same chair, my grandfather found excitement at the thought of such reduced prices. Plus, nothing beat the fact that we were all partaking together. Slightly disappointed that yesterday was not enough, I promptly put back on my "optimism hat," and joined once again for the store's blowout sale.

The following morning, I woke up, sat upright, turned to my mom and dared to ask, "We're going back to Lord & Taylor again, aren't we?"

My mother reluctantly nodded, and I, feeling beaten and exhausted, laid back down in bed as if in denial. Everything was now 70% off, so there we were, once again, as if we had just moved into our new materialistic home. This time, I remember feeling a twinge of concern due to the sketchy behavior of some consumers. Customers were running through the aisles, rummaging the store racks, and acting as though newly infected by some Lord & Taylor disease triggered by retail hysteria. Despite these demonstrations, guess what my family did the next day.

"Now everything is 80% off!" exclaimed my grandfather on Thursday, as if he had learned something entirely new.

This time I felt like I was stuck in some bad dream, *Groundhog Day* style, which involved my inability to ever leave the walls of International Mall's closing complex, and my "optimism hat" was nowhere to be found.

As soon as we entered the store, you could sense how the decrease in prices directly correlated with the increase in worrisome behavior. Consumers were acting as though the end of the world drew near, and only shopping at Lord & Taylor could provide the necessary supplies for survival. Barely anything remained on the racks, so my grandfather left that day having only purchased two pairs of socks. And just like that, the L&T escapade had finally concluded, with every single one of us completely exhausted after what I consider one of the longest weeks of my life. The following morning, I found my grandfather seated at the breakfast table, sharing the news that everything was at 90% off. Thankfully, he refused to support the sale further.

Although exhausting, and somewhat emotionally draining, I love the fact that it happened because one, I can say I'm a Lord & Taylor survivor, and two, because of the precious time the six of us spent together. It is also the perfect example of just how enthusiastic my grandfather was. He saw great joy in even the little things, a trait my beautiful mother most certainly acquired.

For example, one day, the four of us were driving along the highway. Due to the nighttime exhaustion, no one was muttering a sound. Suddenly, my mother emphatically breaks the silence.

"Ijjjjjjjjjh!" she gasped.

My father, swerving the car in response to her abrupt outcry, turned to her with a distressed, "What?!"

*"Miren la luna!* (Translation: Look at the moon!)" She responded, as though she had seen the most life-changing sight.

While the moon might have looked normal to Joe Shmoe, to my mother, it was another miracle of life that had to be celebrated. Was it worth almost losing our lives in a near car collision? Probably not. But to Ana, it meant another incredible mystery to the beauty of the everyday, a moment worth sharing with her dear family.

Because my mother greatly resembled her father, Rafael Felipe Solares, to fully understand my mother, you must know a little bit more about my grandfather.

*"El Abuelo con peluca,"* my uncle Ronald would call her. (Translation: My grandfather with a wig).

My mother loved this statement, because she always aspired to follow in his footsteps, and that she most certainly did.

El Abuelo fervently believed and lived out the ideals of hard work, sacrifice, propriety, knowledge, and to "never, never, give up (Churchill)."

His strong character fueled him to handle all of life's challenges and events elegantly, sowing seeds in everything he touched. His resilience and fascination with excellence led him to building a successful business from the ground up, symbolized by the majestic ash tree he planted years ago, now standing impressively tall, towering over all else in the garden.

As if that was not enough, because of my grandfather's pristine reputation and merit, one day, his friend approached him with the proposition of joining the board of a new bank that was being formed by other great men of the time.

My grandfather stood bewildered and responded, "I don't know anything about banks."

His friend Ramiro responded with, "Neither do I." Nevertheless, they started the bank, and to this day, the bank not only exists, but is also thriving in Latin America.

As a refined gentleman, el Abuelo did enjoy a bit of extravagance every so often in his life. He also, however, thoroughly enjoyed dining at McDonald's with us on road trips and celebrating birthdays at Red Lobster or Carrabba's. It was a beautiful balance of never losing one's elegance while taking pleasure in the simplicities of daily life.

I loved sitting next to my grandfather during shopping outings because I truly believed everything that came out of his mouth was pure gold. From comical comments, to tidbits of history, conversing with my grandfather opened my heart and mind to the cultivation of the whole person. One moment stands out as the inflection point to when my grandfather became more than just a grandfather. It was the moment when el Abuelo and I became great friends.

One day, my family ventured into our beloved neighborhood Target to run a few errands. Shopping at Target usually meant two things for our family: leaving with things you had not intended to purchase in the first place, and time warps. You head in there all jolly and jazzed, with the sunlight still beaming in the 3 p.m. sky, and exit to an inexplicably dark parking lot and a car trunk full of nonsense.

As custom, my grandfather found the first chair he could, and made himself comfortable as he prepared to wait for an inordinate amount of time because, it was Target after all. Resisting the urge to explore the wonders of the toy section, I decided to accompany my grandfather in his sedentary venture. Rather than allowing an unwelcoming silence to settle in, I began to ask Abuelo riddles to keep the conversation interesting.

"What's black and white, and red(read) all over?" I asked, repeating a riddle I heard earlier that day at school. After a respectable amount of time, my grandfather looked to me for the answer.

"The newspaper," I replied.

Now I know I didn't come up with this play on words, but the kind of reaction I received from him made it seem like I had been credited with its conception. I knew I had his attention.

"Why was six afraid of seven?" I asked again. He asked why.

I responded, "Because seven eight (ate) nine."

More laughter and smiles. I continued to share everything I had up my sleeve (thankfully excluding my Greek immigrant bit), enjoying the fact that he took great joy in the same jokes and brain teasers I had the first time I heard them. It was such a fun outing, that before we knew it, everyone else had already returned with their carts full of merchandise, and we experienced a time warp of our own.

Once we made it back to the car, I remember he made a statement regarding our time together.

"I had so much fun with Catherine, she is truly quite something," he said chuckling, with me beaming like a buffoon in the backseat.

That was the beginning of our beautiful friendship, a friendship I would not have had the pleasure in cultivating if it was not for my beautiful Queen. If she hadn't been so close to her parents despite living in the United States, I would have missed out on developing long-lasting friendships with two of the most important people in my life.

Since that day, my grandfather, or *Tricky Bird* as I used to fondly call him, quickly became one of my favorite people.

Quotidian viewings of *Wheel of Fortune* and *Jeopardy*, with me as the scorekeeper, helped strengthen our relationship. The verbal sparring, historical discussions, and jokes that arose throughout the day, especially during the 7 p.m. cocktail hour in his study in Guatemala or in our living room in Tampa, also added to the strength of our bond. The principles we both shared and the values that el Abuelo helped inculcate made us that much closer.

Every morning before school, he would pull me aside and tell me, "Remember Cath, 'Knowledge is Power.'"

I don't know if he understood the magnitude of those words on me, but I held them at the forefront of my life. Every day, I was reminded of how important it was to harness the cultivation of my mind, how I could transform my own future and carve out a path of excellence if I just put forth the effort. I have carried these words with me unceasingly, unlocking happiness and hidden paths as a result.

During the eighteen years in which I had the honor of forming a long-lasting friendship with el Abuelo, he battled tongue cancer. My grandfather was such an incredible and optimistic person, that I never fully comprehended the gravity of the situation. My young age, paired with his upbeat demeanor and quick wit, transformed his visits to Moffitt Cancer Center in Tampa, Florida into pleasant daytime outings filled with great conversations and fine dining. I know what you're thinking, describing hospital food as fine dining may seem like a stretch, but I can sincerely say that the cafeteria at Moffitt became my favorite restaurant because it meant my beloved grandparents were visiting from Guatemala and therefore more laughs and good times were to be had. Plus, I loved their Swedish meatballs.

I enjoyed spending time at Moffitt so much that my beautiful mother would take me out of class so I could tag along. One time in particular serves as the perfect paradigm of this love.

One morning in the fifth grade, I woke up feeling slightly queasy. Not thinking anything of it, I knew I had to go to school because I had a science test to take that morning. My teacher allowed me to take the test earlier than scheduled so I could accompany my mother and grandparents for Abuelo's appointment with Dr. McCaffrey later that afternoon. However, after taking the test, and rushing towards my beautiful mother as she signed me out of school, the nausea intensified. I sat in the car, closed my eyes, and prayed to God that it would subside.

My mother, having always prioritized the wellbeing of her daughters, asked me if I wanted to be taken home due to my pale appearance and unusual silence. Knowing these trips to Moffitt only occurred twice a year, I decided to not take my mother up on her offer and pressed on.

But the nausea only intensified.

Upon entering Moffitt, I did not even make it to the bathroom. I started projectile vomiting into one of the main lobby trash cans like a blacked-out sorority girl. I remember glancing up between my episodes, with my mother behind me holding back my hair. I vaguely remember hearing some sort of singing or instrument playing. Later on, I was told there was a harpist, which at the time of my indisposition, did not provide the usual comfort of a stringed instrument. After about an hour of intermittent sleep, with my 11-year-old body sprawled out across the chairs and my head heavy on my beautiful mother's lap, we made it back home. Turns out, I had the stomach flu, a profound devastation since it deprived me of spending quality time at my favorite restaurant with my favorite people, and consuming Swedish meatballs.

Throughout the subsequent week, I still tried to attend several activities with my family, but every time I tried to make small ranges of motion, the world lost all purpose, except for my toilet. By the third day, however, thinking I, like Jesus, had risen from the dead, joined my family for an Easter classical music concert. Three minutes before it started,

Tequila Tammy from Tri Delta was back in full swing. I ended up in the parking lot, vomiting chicken marsala as though God was smiting me for eating meat on Good Friday. My father was listening to Jim Gaffigan go on about hot pockets all the while.

 Aside from my stomach issues, if my previous story did not convince you of the kind of joy I derived from spending time with my grandparents, perhaps the following phrase will: my favorite Spring Break of all time was during the seventh grade in which I accompanied my grandparents and beautiful mother to the Mayo Clinic. Yes, Spring Break 2008 beats childhood trips to Disney and college excursions in Punta Cana. Yes, our days were filled with doctor appointments. And yes, the hospital was cold and the cafeteria food lacking (in comparison to Moffitt). But the appointments with Dr. David Miller, a prominent radiologist at the Mayo Clinic in Jacksonville, Florida, were quite enjoyable due to his vibrant personality and obvious affection towards his patients, especially my grandfather. (Due to Dr. Miller's genius and the stent they placed in his carotid artery, Dr. Miller extended my grandfather's life several more wonderful years. My family and I are forever indebted to him.)

 Another cause of glee on the trip stemmed from impressing my grandfather with my memory. Dazzled by my brain's ability to recollect snippets of medical terminology, el Abuelo would ask me to bring up particular observations or questions for his consults. It honored me tremendously to aid in the process of ensuring his future health.

 However, the most joy from the trip also came from the moments between the appointments. These include but are not limited to conversations of my future ambitions, discussions of academic topics, readings of human anatomy, composition of limericks, the sharing of jokes during the cocktail hour (Yes, even in the Courtyard Marriott of the Mayo Clinic we honored the daily tradition inclusive of Alex Trebek.) And to cap it all off, watching a rented film with my beautiful Queen in our hotel room before going to sleep. I was truly in Heaven; I was learning; I was helping, and I was with my wonderful mother and her parents. I was having a blast. The. Best. Spring. Break. Ever.

The innate ability for my family to turn worrisome situations into unforgettably joyous occasions still fills me with awe to this day. Rather than dwelling on his cancer, my grandfather lived on, never straying away from the man of faith and character that he was. He continued watching Jeopardy, traveling the world, having cocktail hour every night at 7 p.m., spending time with his family, and enjoying the richness of his life until the very end. A gentleman, a scholar, a dreamer, and a doer. Doesn't get much better than that.

Just as I am fascinated with my mother, my mother was fascinated with her father. El Abuelo was her favorite person, just as my mother was mine. The similar tendencies and life beliefs the three of us shared created a bond, which I still feel even after all these years. I thank God every day for this connection, because it always reminds me of the strength I know I have within me and the life I know I am meant to lead.

*My mother holding me as
my sister ponders her new life.*

CHAPTER FOUR

# Marvelous Mom

*May God bless you yesterday, today, and tomorrow.*

**NOVEMBER 10, 2017**

When Ana Young is your mother, the question of whether to submit her photo to the Marvelous Mom Contest was a no-brainer. "And the winner of this year's Marvelous Mom Contest goes to… " I could hear each word reverberate with hopeful anticipation as Mrs. VP spoke into the microphone. Would my mother be chosen for this great honor? Would the years of countless hours spent as Homeroom Mother, Girl Scout Chaperone, and Junior Ring Ceremony cake extraordinaire finally pay off?

Regardless of the outcome, as if in a flash of light, I began to envision all the reasons why she deserved this title.

There is a reason why I fostered such a strong relationship with my grandparents. They were the two principal individuals who shaped my beautiful mother's persona. She learned how to love and become an impeccable pillar of unwavering support, a caregiver beyond the norm. She was beguiled by intellectual curiosity, but most importantly she was entranced by love, her motherly love and support she never ceded.

I'm not talking about your standard "I left my lunch at home and she'd come back to school to bring it for me" type of support. Rather, I'm talking about "jumping into the community pool fully clothed with an unfastened wig to save my life" kind of backing.

I'm referring to a kind of support that goes beyond the ordinary tasks of life, far beyond something Maslow in his Hierarchy of Needs could have ever imagined. The kind that just makes you wonder what you did to deserve this depth of love and attention. The kind that inspires you to excel and reach far beyond normal capacity.

It all started when I was a little girl. My mother would situate herself in between both our beds and extend her arms to hold our hands as my sister and I fell asleep, singing soft lullabies all the while. It was no easy task, especially since I used to be plagued by frequent nightmares which prevented me from quickly dozing off. But my sweet mother never stopped holding our hands until we were both deep in slumber, despite her inevitable arm pain of an unprecedented aerobic exercise.

As I became older, my fear level at night persisted, and I regularly asked my beautiful Queen to sit with me as I fell asleep due to the unquantifiable peace her presence provided.

One night, to further calm my nerves, my mother sweetly stated, "You know Cath, I have to tell you something."

My heart sank. What was she going to say?

She continued, "I don't know how to tell you this, but… I'm an angel."

Now you'd think my reaction at such news would resemble that of a recently converted atheist who had just witnessed a blinding light on his way to Damascus. On the contrary, my head began to flood with existential questions that saturated my body with even more fear.

"How is this possible? How was I born? Is my mother actually my mother? Can angels have children? Who is this person sitting in front of me? Where is my actual mother?" I asked myself silently and fearfully, managing to somehow feel weak at the knees in a supine position.

My mother, picking up on my concern and realizing her plan of support had backfired, stifled the crisis by retracting her previous statement.

"No Cath, I'm not an angel. I just wanted to provide you with peace in knowing that God and his angels will never abandon you," she sweetly redacted.

That night, I still barely slept. Entertaining the idea, even for a moment, that my beautiful mother was not actually my earthly mother was enough to prevent me from attaining a month's worth of adequate respite. Regardless, I know everything my mother did was done in good faith and with the best intentions. Today, I smile at the situation because unbeknownst to me at the time, she truly was and always will be my guardian angel. How blessed am I?

And so, I learned to become truly dependent on my mother. So much so, that when I was about five years old, I did something no daughter ever should… I made my parents cut short their two-week Hawaiian vacation. I realize now that I quite skillfully earned the title "Worst Daughter of the Year" faster than any pubescent adolescent ever could. But I couldn't help it. To be separated from the most wonderful person on this planet for two whole weeks? Not a chance.

So, there I was, every day, calling long-distance from my grandparents' phone in Guatemala in a panic with my Minnie Mouse calendar, marking down the days until their arrival.

If the responses to my questioning were unsatisfactory, I asserted rather matter-of-factly, "No Mommy, you told me you were arriving on the 17th," pointing at the date I alone determined with my *Hercules* themed marker.

To home in on my argument, I concluded each phone call with the grand finale, the crux of my argument, *"Es que, es que… I love you."* (Translation: "It's just that, it's just that… I love you).

My voice shaken, but my victory imminent.

Every day was like this. I could not be convinced, despite several family members' attempts. They even tried to win me over with different foods and treats, a strategy that usually provided *fruitful* results. But no number of brownies from *Paiz* or chicken nuggets from *Pollo Campero* could thwart my stance on the issue at hand. I needed my Mommy like I needed to breathe.

And alas, my parents came home a week earlier than they had originally anticipated.

I genuinely believe only Ana Young would find it in her heart to pay *extra* money in flight changes to spend less time on a worry-free vacation in paradise. But my mother always put me and my sister first, no matter the circumstance or cost.

*Disclaimer: to this day, I still apologize to my father and grandmother for my actions and for any pain, both emotional and physiological, I might have caused.*

---

Another testament to my mother's unparalleled support was our hair. My sister's and my hair were no match for the jungle gym because my mother blew dry our hair every single day. So, no matter how many times I jumped off the swing, hung upside down on the monkey bars, or fell down the slide, my hair would always fall back into place due to the time and care my mother spent on it. I remember my friends in grade school used to marvel at the phenomenon of my unmarred mane post-recess.

I recall my friend Devin Allen commenting, "How does your hair always look so perfect?"

The answer was simple: Mom.

In addition to the long hours spent styling, my beautiful mother adorned our hair with large bows that looked more like an extension of giant heads due to their sheer magnitude. These bows, however, were so precious to our mother, that when one of them got lost, Ana would stop at nothing to find them. She would have security guards search the perimeter of our local shopping complex, make restaurant hosts interrogate staff both in and out of the kitchen, press hotel management to inspect corridors and closets. The bows could not remain lost, usually becoming an all-out manhunt in which both family and nonfamily members would partake.

Why go through all the trouble for a piece of headwear you may ask? In the world of Ana Young, those bows exemplified all the effort my mother was willing to put in for me and my sister so that we always felt and looked out best. They symbolized her generosity, as well as the values of hard work, ethics, and elegance.

Simply put, the price she paid for extra-large bows was no small fee and she wanted the best for her daughters.

One of my favorite stories underscoring my mother's incessant support dates to around seven years ago in 2015. Our family was in Antigua, Guatemala for Holy Week, as was custom since I was a little girl. One day, we were all relaxing poolside, waiting for lunch to be served. One member of the group started making absent-minded observations regarding strengths and weaknesses of those present. When I found myself as the object of such scrutiny, I was completely confounded by the resulting conclusion: I was somehow lacking readiness for life. According to this individual, there were plenty of qualities and traits I needed to work on to achieve an optimal level of maturity. I know what you're thinking… who would pass unsought-for judgment so freely besides poorly trained therapists? To be fair, the individual was completely right. I was not even ready to fill a prescription at the pharmacy, let alone tackle the complications of adulthood. Regardless, the words stung, so I paid a visit to my usual source of comfort. Upon disclosing the conversation to My Queen, peppered with the inevitable demonstration of tears as I uttered words between breaths, I found great console in my mother's unending wisdom, accompanied by the sheer perfection of her embrace.

The power of an Ana Young hug can only be described as a display of magnificence.

About two hours later, I was approached by the culprit in the corridor of my grandmother's house. With a tangible aura of guilt and a defeated tone in voice, the individual asked for forgiveness, expressing deep regret in the effects of the words shared.

I was taken aback. How did this person know I was struggling with the statements made and the conclusions drawn? The only explanation I could produce was that the person overheard my conversation with my beautiful mother. And so, panic set in, and I worried that my relationship with this person had been compromised due to my "tattling."

It was not until recently I learned my mother had gone to confront the individual about what was said, in her *can I speak to the manager*-fashion. She sternly, yet lovingly corrected the person's facts to squelch future proclamations.

Learning that it was my incredible mother who stepped in to save the day made me feel overwhelmed with appreciation for her unending support. No one could mess with me or my sister. If they did, Mama Young would stop at nothing to protect us, always ensuring our safety and happiness.

This protection included the artform of waking up. My mother, every morning before school, would sweetly wake me and my sister up by gently tapping our arm, kissing our cheek, and sweetly saying, "It's time to wake up, *mi muchachita*."

Despite the pain of a 6:30 a.m. wake up call, I remember commencing the day with a sense of calm due to the tenderness with which she awoke me. I cannot say the same when my father rolled in at six.

First, a rather loud rendition of "Heigh Ho" from *Snow White and the Seven Dwarfs* aggravated my dreamlike state, followed by a series of indefensible blows to the face by the unused pillow on my left.

Hoping to end the cushion combat, I contested by screaming, "Mommy!!!"

Within the minute, my greatest line of defense arrived, and the pillow perpetrator was promptly put in place.

Her care and protection extended beyond outside forces and materialized in basic goods, such as toothpaste. So much toothpaste. My beautiful mother always provided us with an inordinate amount of dental cream, so much so, that our family should own Procter & Gamble stock. So much toothpaste I could probably change my daily routine to brushing eight times a day and still come out with a three-year supply. Not only was my mother a shepherdess of love, she was also the number one supplier of basic life essentials.

"*My Mommy, ya no necesito más pasta de dientes,* (Translation: My Mommy, I don't need any more toothpaste)," I would state, in the most loving way possible, pointing to my impressive collection of hygienic products.

Her usual response was as follows, *"Yo se mijita, pero mas vale que sobre!* (Translation: I know my daughter, but it's better to have more than enough than not enough").

The collection did not stop at teeth cleansing products. The number of Dove bars of soap I always had overflowed from my bathroom cabinet to the drawers underneath the sink. Toilet paper? Never lacking. Tissue boxes? Fully stocked. This abundance of toiletries is testament to her preoccupation of ensuring we always had enough of everything. At the beginning, the plethora of product caused frustration due to the cumbersome process of storage. But I learned to appreciate this act of providing, so characteristic of a mother who wanted nothing but to give her daughters everything.

You can imagine when I went away to college. I can guarantee I was the only resident at Notre Dame to own ten packs of dental floss at a time. I'm also certain no one else came back from shopping at CVS with thirteen bags of merchandise and a receipt the size of my comforter. But that was Mom, illustrating a rare and deep love that only my sister and I experienced. The miracle of Mom that kept our lives so whole and so pure. The miracle that gave me everything.

Perhaps one of the reasons for all the toothpaste is that my mother used to let my sister and me consume packets of sugar at restaurants when we were little. Not wanting us to feel suppressed or sad in any way when we were children, whenever we would ask for permission to eat the sugar, my mother gave the go ahead. My father, on the other hand, did not share the same sentiments, and thus contested every time we merrily took our first step towards early-onset diabetes. But no one, not even my father, could overturn an Ana Young decision. She wanted our happiness, and if that meant temporarily risking our pancreatic health, then so be it. What's life without a little sugar anyway, right?

<hr />

Beyond the realm of over-the-counter products and sugar packets, my mother always had the foresight of ensuring my sister and I were prepared for the future. This includes purchasing a 24-person set of Williams Sonoma Thanksgiving china for *each* of us. My poor grandmother suffered the brunt of such a purchase because for years, we used her room as storage. I could never forget the day, which unknowingly turned into night, when we were shopping in Williams Sonoma. Thinking we were simply going to buy two jars of their butternut squash soup, we left the shop with not one, but two cars full of merchandise later that evening (my father had to drive in to provide his automobile for extra transport). Everything she bought that day (besides the soup), however, was for her daughters and our future homes. Now, let it be known, that my sister and I were nowhere near getting married or having houses of our own (well, if you don't count my sister's "marriage" to Mr. Q). But that didn't matter. My mother was a visionary and knew that one day, we would profit from such dinnerware.

My incredible mother's support also extended to the content she was comfortable with her daughters becoming exposed to on television.

"You only want to watch shows and movies that are going to fill your mind with good things," she would say as we flipped through channels.

So naturally a show about a large, talking, extinct purple creature that sang songs and played games with real children made the cut.

Barney in our house was a celebrity. We owned numerous VHS tapes, knew all the songs, and of course, "never let the water run" when we brushed our teeth or washed our hands. So admired was the dinosaur in our family that when we took a trip to Universal Studios with my grandparents, my beautiful mother and Abuela became overwhelmed with emotion and started crying at the mere sight of Barney. I remember feeling an extreme sense of bewilderment, sprinkled with a dash of embarrassment, feelings I'm sure my father and grandfather both shared. Here were two fully grown women, fangirling a children's sitcom star more so than his juvenile spectators.

In retrospect, I can absolutely see why they were overtaken by such sentiment. Barney provided my sister and I with valuable life lessons at a critical age. For example, my personal favorite song went something like this, "Just imagine, just imagine, just imagine all the things that we could be. Imagine all the places we could go and see. Imagination's fun for you and me." Not only is the melody harmonious, but the message it sends to children of the importance of dreams is something quite beautiful and irreplaceable, characteristic of other Barney ballads. And so, my mother's and grandmother's tears were that of joy and gratitude for Barney's guidance in our early lives.

Another show my mother supported us watching was *Gilmore Girls*. Not only did the main character, Rory a highly motivated individual with aspirations of attending a prestigious university, set a good example, but also the beautiful relationship she held with her mother, Lorelai, made the show that much more appealing. So many times, movies and television shows portray a fragmented relationship between teenage girls and their mothers. My mother loved that *Gilmore Girls* gave a fresh perspective on the special bond between a mother and daughter. And thus, every day at 5 p.m., we would watch the show together, my mother commenting on the grandparents' beautiful home and Emily's St. John's outfits all the while. It was absolute Heaven being able to share those moments with her. I'm just glad we never stumbled across Alexis Bledel or Lauren Graham, or else another Barney-related crying fest would have inevitably taken place.

When it came to movies, if my mother discovered a film that

inculcated positive life lessons or sentiments, she stopped at nothing to ensure my sister and I saw it. For example, my mother watched the movie *Leap Year* twice in twenty-four hours, once with me in the morning and then again in the evening with me and my sister. Because she wanted *both* of her daughters to benefit from a beautiful movie, she didn't mind watching the same motion picture twice in one day. Unfortunately, that led me to partake in the duplicate viewing; but, if it meant spending more time with my happy Queen, then I was on board.

All throughout grade school, the kind of motherly agency I received included hours of her sitting down with me as I completed homework. Every history assignment and every spelling exercise had to be completed cleanly and accurately. She would even read chapters with me, placing emphasis on every comma so I would learn when to use them.

"Fortunately 'COMMA,' the United States was successful in their efforts 'COMMA,'" my mother would recite from my history book, placing more importance on the comma than on our American victory.

I am convinced that because of this practice, every year for our school's standardized test I received a perfect score in punctuation. It is also the reason why I received a perfect score of 36 on the ACT in the English section.

One moment stands out as a perfect example of the kind of scholarly backing I always felt growing up, the support that helped fuel me to do my best in everything I did. It was a normal Monday in the fifth grade. I attended school, went to volleyball practice, came home, spent the entire afternoon doing homework, and prepared for bed. As I started to doze off, a shot of adrenaline raced through my body. I suddenly realized I had a religion quiz the following day, and I had not prepared for it in the slightest. It was already 10 p.m., which for an eleven-year-old might as well be two in the morning. In a panic, I turned on all my lights and frantically searched my backpack for my textbook, which I could not find due to the blur of my tears. Upon witnessing the commotion, my mother and father both entered the room and asked what was going on.

I explained the situation, and without hesitation, they both sat down with me and said, almost in unison, "Do not worry. We are going to help you."

And so, after hugging them and allowing myself to have a good cry, the three of us read the designated chapters, and studied for approximately two hours, despite my father's insistence on answering "Jesus" to every question. Once I felt comfortable with the material, I fell asleep, aced the quiz, and all was well with the world again. In that very moment, I knew exactly how blessed I was to have that kind of support from both of my parents.

This parental crutch was also very evident in the Academy's Elementary School Talent Show, which became hours long of practice to perfect choreographed routines, with massive colorful balloons lining the stage as my sister and I danced to "Up, Up, and Away" by The Fifth Dimension, a song from the 60s no one except for a handful of teachers were familiar with, or "Miracles Happen" from the movie *The Princess Diaries.* My father oversaw the choreography, and my mother oversaw set design and wardrobe, usually from Limited Too. Looking back upon old videos, I am sad to say I am not the kind of dance professional I thought I was whilst performing our carefully crafted programs. I looked more like an overzealous tribal leader, preparing the village for an upcoming famine. Regardless of our actual talent, The Young sisters performances became legendary and are still talked about today.

My beautiful mother was so caring that she always wanted us to have pets of our own so we too could learn from a young age how to properly look after other beings. Before our dog, we had a pet baby chick. Unfortunately, the chick did not receive as much love as our dear Millie, soiling and damaging multiple pieces of furniture everywhere she went. And thus, when the soiling became too much and the chick began to grow, my parents decided it was time to take her to a farm.

When the owners asked my Queen what we had named the little creature, my mother, not knowing what to respond, returned with, "Chicken."

My father, holding back an outburst of laughter, hoped to save the awkward situation by changing her answer to "McChicken."

Now I don't know which is worse... not naming our pet chicken or naming it after the byproduct of its recently deceased cousin. Regardless, "Chicken" had to go.

After the chick, we had multiple fish, usually Betta fish and tadpoles we'd collect in a nearby pond. However, one day we decided it was a good idea to have the species intermingle. You can imagine the bloodbath that ensued when Rainbow, our Betta fish, asserted dominance over the poor tadpoles. Not one survived. Despite the trauma of losing our aquatic pets due to Darwinist principles, my sister and I always insisted on having a dog.

When Ana Young is your mother, you adopt a furry, monochromatic sister who like you, tends to consume everything and anything. My beautiful Queen was not only the best mother to me and my sister, she was also the best mother to our beautiful Chihuahua, Millie (short for Millennium since we purchased her in the year 2000). Millie was with our family for an amazing eighteen years. Yes, you read that correctly. If Millie were human, she could have voted. She even could have joined the military. Every year we celebrated her birthday, usually baking her a cake in the shape of a bone and placing a birthday hat atop her small head for three seconds before she inevitably protested. I am convinced that Millie lasted as long as she did due to the love and food, most times in excess, that my mother gave her day in and day out. Sometimes, my mom fed her cereal, made her a small pancake, and even gave her a small portion of eggs. She truly owned and morphed into her human persona, and we loved her dearly.

Millie was not just a dog; she was my sister. She was the third furry daughter that left behind a trail of hairs no matter where she went. She was sassy yet confident, knowing how much my mother cared for her. She had her own wardrobe, costumes for several occasions, and monogrammed blankets and beds. She was even bilingual. She responded to both English and Spanish, impressing my beautiful mother every time with her intellectual dexterity. She truly lived the life, spending all day with my mom, sometimes running errands with her, and picking us up from school. My mother loved Millie beyond words. She was so grateful to our sweet dog for keeping her company while my father was at work and my sister and I were in school. It was a love affair like no other.

Millie would even travel to Guatemala with us for Christmas and summer vacations, an ordeal that required a stop in Miami to secure paperwork with the Department of Agriculture and the Guatemalan consulate. But nothing was too difficult or complex if it meant we could spend our two-week vacation with our smallest, yet eldest family member.

Days when we could stay at home from school not only meant we could spend more time with Millie, but also with Ana Young. I don't think I would properly convey the concept of how supportive my mother was without mentioning the hallowed activity of becoming ill. Yes, sick days were gifts from God (except for the Moffitt harpist & hot pocket episodes). To be taken care of by Ana Young was like having a parade in your honor; you were the star and received plenty of gifts and attention without putting in any effort. Despite not feeling physically well in the slightest, I experienced an overwhelming joy to be granted the honor of staying home with my beautiful Queen!

Thankfully, it was a two-way street of excitement, apparent in the level of worry regarding my slight fever and her subsequent plea for asking me to stay.

If I was ever unsure about whether I should go to school, my mother would always sternly respond with, *"No Cath, mejor quedase y cuidase. Se puede poner peor!"* (Translation: No Cath, it's better if you stay and take care of yourself. You could get worse!).

Based on her reaction and adamancy, you would have thought I had just been diagnosed with tuberculosis rather than a common cold. But that was My Mommy. Always looking out for me and my overall wellbeing, making me feel happy and comfortable despite all circumstances.

If my mother was happy having us home when we were not feeling our best, imagine the joy during summer vacations. Some parents view summers as a jubilant time with their children but await the day when the annual period ends to gain back some normalcy in their day-to-day lives. A *Staples* commercial a few years ago depicted this concept perfectly. It portrayed a mother and father shopping for school supplies singing the song "It's the Most Wonderful Time of the Year," dancing down the aisles of a Staples store all the while. Rather than referring to Christmastime, the parents in the advertisement were thrilled their children were returning to school.

My mother found this commercial quite hilarious because she could not relate to these kinds of parents. I remember her palpable sadness as summer ended, dreading the day her girls would have to leave home again and move forward with their scholastic obligations away from home. Mornings of watching *Pet Star* with Mario Lopez and *The Nanny* with Fran Fine and Mr. Sheffield, while eating Cinnamon Toast Crunch permeate my mind as some of the happiest moments of my life. Weekend trips to the Trade Winds at St. Pete Beach during which we would sleep in, eat her deliciously prepared "coditos" or pasta salad, and watch *Shark Week* as an ironic gesture after having spent all day in the water, take the prize as some of my most joyous memories. That feeling of warmth on Sunday mornings, when my father would blast "Cherish" by The Association throughout the house, claiming it was the "greatest song ever written," as my mother prepared pancakes and omelets, *egging* him on to change the music to classical. Trips to Guatemala where we tightened up our Spanish-speaking abilities, celebrating every day with delicious food and precious moments with family members. The nights in Antigua where the four of us would listen to music, taking in the warmth of the fireplace in our nighttime refuge of the corner room. My mother went above and beyond, making our summer breaks remarkable. Truly a quintessential mother whose adoration for her daughters extended beyond the norm.

"And the winner of this year's Marvelous Mom goes to... Ana Young," Mrs. VP announced, followed by a great roar and applause from the audience, and an especially emphatic one from me and my sister. Because the annual Mother Daughter Dinner was hosted by Student Council, a student organization my sister and I were both a part of, we were even given the great honor of handing her the sash and flowers, an impressive arrangement my mother purchased herself since I oversaw procuring the bouquet as a member of the event's planning committee.

To win Marvelous Mom, daughters in the senior class submit photos of their mothers when they were in high school. Then, the whole school votes for whom they believe is the most marvelous based on the picture and preceding reputation. She won the honor, out of all the moms in my sister's senior class (roughly about ninety) not only because our mother was incredibly stunning in high school, but also the effort, love, and cuteness my mom was well known for made her the top candidate in this longstanding tradition. It was as if the culmination of all her efforts as a mother at the Academy of the Holy Names took shape in this great honor, with my sister and I beaming, as we handed her the prize.

I could not think of anyone more deserving.

*My darling mother with
her fall festive garb.*

CHAPTER FIVE

# The Beauty is in the Details

*Qué alegre!*

JUNE 24, 2004

When Ana Young is your mother, the word "detail" takes on a whole new meaning. Every trip back home from college led to unanticipated gestures, ranging from abounding bouquets of flowers to folded ends of toilet paper resembling the protocol of a five-star hotel.

If the beauty is in the detail, imagine how much beauty there was when the detail was orchestrated by Ana Young, the most beautiful lady that ever graced our lives.

One of my first memories of the whimsy of an Ana Young detail was one afternoon when I was around three or four years old. My sister and I took a nap with our darling mother in her bed. Before falling asleep, she stated she had a surprise for us when we awoke. My sister and I eagerly went to sleep with a feeling synonymous to Christmas Eve. When 5 p.m. hit, I remember waking up to the most incredible smell. She had made us cinnamon and sugar toast, a snack she also grew up consuming. I remember feeling the warmth of our dear home so profoundly in that moment, not because of the heat radiating from the oven-cooked buttery creations, but because I felt an all-consuming bliss in the happy quarters my mother fostered.

She created this wonderful home through the details that pervaded our everyday lives.

Not even natural disasters were excluded from the details of Ana Young. Hurricane days became themed celebrations involving music, movies, buffets of food, and decorations to keep morale high. "Today, we are going to have Mexican food," revealed my beautiful Queen regarding the day's cultural focus, apparent by the dining table's décor. The next day, Italian, the day after that, Chinese, and so on. I remember the second Bay News 9 flashed the notice that schools in Hillsborough County were closing the next day, an immediate song and dance would break out among the four of us. Not only did we celebrate the fact that we would all be together in the comfort of our beautiful home with an Ana Young fiesta on the horizon, but also due to the fun family sleepovers that took place because of the impending natural disaster, requiring continual parental presence.

And so it was, every June to November. Despite the inclement weather outside, there was so much joy emanating from Ana Young inside, that hurricane season became a close second to Christmas. Not your usual Floridian storm story.

Another event infused with the spirit of Ana Young revolves around the celebration of the century, aka my sister's and my First Holy Communion carnival. You read that right, our own private carnival.

In a ceremonious conviviality, my mother arranged a mini carnival in my grandparents' backyard to celebrate my sister's and my coming of age in the Catholic religion. There was a miniature Ferris wheel, cotton candy machine, booths with different games to win prizes, a magic show, and of course, the religious ceremony that took place in my grandparents' in-house chapel. For those of you foreign to Catholicism, this is not normal. Usually, after the Mass, families will celebrate by going to eat lunch at their friendly neighborhood Olive Garden where they consume endless soup, salad, and breadsticks.

But not in the world of Ana Young. Instead, we got to eat lunch after the Hispanic-looking Criss Angel awarded me and my sister bunny rabbits out of his hat.

    I kid you not when I say that this First Communion extravaganza is talked about in Guatemala to this very day. I can't express the number of times friends of my parents have come up to me and mentioned, not the fact that I had seen them at a function a year prior, but the fact that they were there for my First Holy Communion. Some people still have the party favor mugs with our faces on them. Talk about a conversation piece.

---

    You can imagine the details present in birthdays. When Ana Young is your mother, your first-grade homeroom class receives individual, beautifully decorated, mini-birthday cakes in your honor. Yes, that's right. Instead of store-bought cupcakes or brownies, my classmates received their very own "Happy Birthday Catherine Anne" fondant-covered confection. My academic peers quickly learned to love my mom after having had such an opportunity to indulge, since the cakes pushed the boundary of what constituted a normal first grader's serving size.

    Birthdays in the eyes of Ana Young were sacred. They were never viewed as a perfunctory passing of time. Rather, they were always celebrated as a victory in the game of life. Another year of birth meant another year of the gift of life.

    Every birthday had a special component. Whether it was a unique present, a charming card with my mother's calligraphy-like handwriting, a memorable restaurant, or a large jubilee, everything was thought up by the walking angel herself. A few highlights include my seventh birthday celebration at Busch Gardens, my thirteenth birthday party catered by Starbucks, with a cake in the shape of a present so extravagantly large, that not even my collective seventh grade constituency could ever dream of finishing (apparently large cakes were a common theme in my life), and my twenty-first birthday observance in New York for New Year's. My sister also had her fair share of birthday celebrations, including her thirteenth Hawaiian Luau, a surprise seventeenth birthday party at the majestic Don Cesar in St. Petersburg Beach, and her twenty-first birthday dinner inside the Eiffel Tower in Paris.

The word "wealthy" may pop into your head as the reason behind each detail's execution. However, as a homemaker and wife of a military officer, my mother certainly broke the mold with all she did within her means. With her creativity and grace, and her vast familiarity with the art of couponing, no ambition was ever stifled, and no birthday was left uncelebrated.

One birthday stands out as the pinnacle of all my annual jubilations. For most birthdays, I would ask for two things: cookie cake and a trip to Disney. My father usually contested one of these requests. (Hint: it was not the option that cost $12.99.) But, with the powerful persuasion of Ana Young, we were back in the sanctuary of the Magic Kingdom come December.

On my ninth birthday, we took the routine trip to Disney, commencing with the standard Disney twirl and cry (not the whimper from my father after every purchase), rather the burst of emotion upon seeing the Christmas decorations line up towards the castle. The morning was filled with parades and laughter, delectable food, and diverting rides. Oh, how happy I was to be back!

"The only thing that could be missing is cookie cake," I remember commenting to My Queen as we headed down Main Street to make our way towards Space Mountain.

Yes, I was the worst. It wasn't enough that we were at Disney. I had to have cookie cake, like the plump Augustus Gloop child I was, itching to dive into a chocolate river at any given time.

"That reminds me, we need to go pick it up at a bakery in Fantasyland at 4 p.m.!" The Queen stated, as if by the happiest royal decree.

As a Disney expert, I remember standing bewildered at the comment, for it was news to me that there was a bakery in Fantasyland to fulfill such requests. But, because it involved cookie cake, I didn't ask follow-up questions and proceeded to happily skip towards my chocolate dream.

As 4 p.m. drew near, however, I started to get slightly anxious, fearing chocolate chunk deprivation. I mean, it is cookie cake after all.

"It is chocolate chip cookie cake, right? With frosting and everything?" I interrogated as though it was their first time celebrating my birthday.

Avoiding my insolent questioning, as we made our way to the mysterious bakery, my mother suddenly stopped. Confused, I began looking around at where we were standing, trying to find an explanation as to why our cookie quest came to an abrupt halt. I will never forget the beautiful smile from my mother's perfect face as I began to realize we were standing underneath Cinderella's Castle, next to the restaurant hostess stand. We both immediately began to shed an impressive amount of tears. Even more than the cries from my father, the emotion was so palpable that passers-by probably believed I was an adopted child who had just been reunited with her birth mom.

I will never forget the embrace that followed, with my fairy Godmother of a mom, having achieved something more impressive than turning a pumpkin into a horse-drawn carriage. She fulfilled my childhood dream of dining inside Cinderella's Castle with Cinderella herself.

About a month prior to this event, my beautiful mother asked me if there was anything else I would want to celebrate my ninth year of life. Knowing full-well how far-fetched it was, I reluctantly mentioned my ideal dining location. A week later, I brought up the subject once more, and asked my miraculous mother if she was able to secure a reservation.

She responded melancholically, "I called, but they said we have to make a reservation six months in advance, and even then, they can't confirm we'd have it. I'm so sorry, my Cath."

In actuality, my mother called every day for a month straight, captivating each of the Disney Reservations' employees with her charm, compelling them to eventually grant her wish. And just like that, the magic of Ana Young was restored, and the birthday dinner produced an unforgettable memory. And yes, the day still ended with cookie cake.

Of all her details, some of the most memorable centered around holidays. For example, for Valentine's Day, my sister and I would receive stuffed animals and chocolates with a handwritten card expressing her undying love for us since we were five. You can imagine my father's confusion the first time he had to share this widely accepted romantic holiday with his two daughters. But despite the paternal perplexity, every year, my mother could not help but include us in her unique celebration of love.

Another example was Halloween. Rather than occurring one day a year, Halloween was a daily collection of surprises for the entire month of October. "Every day, you are going to receive something special in your pumpkin bag outside your door," shared my beautiful Queen in her festive orange Ralph Lauren blouse. Unlike Valentine's Day, this tradition started when I was twenty-two. No age was off limits to the magic.

I would be remiss if I didn't mention Thanksgiving, and the subsequent burden of distributing annual Panera Holiday Breads to every teacher and faculty member at our school. Yes, you read that correctly. Every year, my mother would buy as many as twenty-four Holiday Breads, each with a bag of its own and a handwritten note.

One year in particular led to a rather confusing turn of events. On the day of my obligatory disbursement, usually two days leading up to the national day of family and feast, Mrs. McKevanny pulls me aside during my third-grade religion class and states in a matter-of-fact fashion, "Tell your mother, there's no shoe."

Now, Mrs. McKevanny and I got along just fine, usually with our lines of communication free from confusion.

The message was so cryptic, however, that I inevitably probed further, "What do you mean, 'There's no shoe?'" I responded with a concerned inflection, questioning now Mrs. McKevanny's sanity altogether.

"Tell her, there's no shoe," she repeats again, this time as though she just uttered an irreversible truth.

"No shoe?" I asked in a final attempt at understanding.

"Yes, no shoe," she responds.

So, despite losing focus for the rest of the school day in an attempt to crack the code, I relayed the message to my mother as soon as I saw her.

"So, My Mommy, Mrs. McKevanny told me to tell you that there's no shoe...?" Almost immediately, my mother bursts into the most genuine and contagious form of laughter.

Turns out, my mom had a pair of old smelly shoes she wanted to have fixed by a local cobbler, but she couldn't find one of the shoes after having dropped me and my sister off with our large bags filled with Panera bread. In an initial panic, my beautiful mother feared that the lost, foul-smelling shoe would turn up in a teacher's gift bag; she proceeded to call each recipient to ensure the bread remained unharmed by the perilous footwear. Apparently, my mother had found the shoe hours later underneath one of the seats of our Ford Expedition.

So, Mrs. McKevanny's message finally made sense, her sanity authenticated, and the bread? Unscathed.

So why go through all that trouble of calling all the teachers and even bothering with holiday breads in the first place? Ana Young was so special and extraordinary that she truly wanted to give back to those individuals that were essentially caring for her daughters in her absence. It was her way of ensuring the teachers knew the strength of our familial bond and the depth of her motherly love for both me and my sister, sprinkled with her unending generosity so characteristic of the season. However, to this very day, when Thanksgiving rolls around, I still thank God that there was, in fact, no shoe.

---

Of all the holidays, however, Christmas was by far the most celebrated.

I am known by most as the embodiment of Christmas cheer, a human incarnate of *holly jolly* with Buddy the Elf as my spirit animal (also attributed to my frequent consumption of large maple syrup servings).

Aside from my high sugar diet, I have always believed in the following truth: Christmas is not just a time of year; rather, it is a way of life. The joy and laughter, the kindness towards others, the brightness of celebration… all these things distinctive to the latter half of the year can be and *should* be practiced year-round.

As with most things in my life, this love and introspection stems from my mother. And as with most things, her love of Christmas surpassed the norm.

She loved her sweaters, festive jewelry, and even hats. She would fill our house with so many poinsettias, it was as if our lives depended on them for oxygen. And despite the height of our ceilings, she always insisted on purchasing the tallest evergreen conifer in the lot, a smell that proliferated our home even after our annual trip to Guatemala.

Imagine the gifts she would give me and my sister.

Every Nochebuena, the Latin American celebration of Christmas Eve, my sister and I received about five or six presents *more* than our cousins. This was despite being the only family members who had to travel from a different country, having to transport all presents in suitcases. And no, we never traveled lightly.

It was truly a spectacle to see so many gifts wrapped under my grandmother's spectacular tree. Even if they were small, like lip gloss or themed socks, she would wrap them up individually so that we felt special in opening numerous gifts.

One year, she gave us a gift that only a detail-oriented mother would ever give. She gave my sister and I our own My Twinn Doll, that is a doll that looked exactly like us, even with what they were wearing.

I think my mother was more excited about seeing our reactions towards such a thoughtful gift than we were to receive the dolls. I know I definitely was not the model daughter in my reaction, for that doll proceeded to cause me great emotional trauma.

Imagine having a lifelike grimacing figurine of yourself watch your every move as a little girl, sometimes falling inexplicably and at times, moving to different places. The latter part was largely attributed to my father's genius as a source of paternal entertainment, where he would purposefully move the doll to give it the semblance of consciousness. However, I did not learn this until years later when the psychological detriment had run its course.

The stories I also used to hear at sleepovers or Girl Scouts also heightened my fear of "The Doll." I became so afraid that I even learned how to sleep with my legs bent in an upwards position to block Marionette Catherine's frightful gaze towards me.

And so, as I got older, I begged my parents to get rid of the doll to restore some bedroom peace. However, after periods of time, I would find my request of disposal had not yet been fulfilled, discovering my angry-looking porcelain-self tucked away somewhere.

"In the future your fear will pass, and you will be thankful you kept her," my mother would plead, rationalizing why she made the decision to keep my childhood doll.

To this day, I am still uneasy regarding the uncertainty of her presence in the house, refusing to even bring the topic into conversation.

Now this complex relationship towards such a beautiful gift-giving gesture was one of the few disagreements I held with my mother. But despite its effects, I thank her fully for taking the time and energy to invest in such a thoughtful gift, done solely out of the goodness of her beautiful heart.

The magic of an Ana Young Christmas even extended to corporate America. During my first year with General Mills, I decided to offer my neighborhood's community clubhouse for our region's annual holiday party. Knowing my mother's knack for organizing unforgettable festivities, coupled with my love of the season, I knew I was well-equipped for fulfilling the party's vision. My boss and mentor, Scott Nevitt, oversaw side dishes, Adam George, my coworker, was in charge of overall execution, including ascertaining and assembling serving stations and high-top tables, and I had miscellaneous decorating and the overall procurement of the space. When disclosing my position to my mother, she immediately cranked the holiday spirit tenfold and decided to take my plans for moderate Christmas décor into overdrive. Not only did she purchase twenty plus poinsettias out of pocket, she also had a professional present-shaped cake made at Publix, with the words "Happy Holidays" spread across next to our logo. As expected, it was large enough to feed four times the number of people in attendance. Another large cake to *frost* our memory.

She also decided to buy little bags of our cereal products to use as ornaments on the Christmas tree in the middle of the gathering area. Her vision turned our small gathering into the corporate party of the century, and people to this day still talk about the cake and the genius behind the ornaments.

As a detail-oriented individual, my mother took the mundane and transformed it into a talking piece for months on end. She was able to enjoy the joys of the present that much more due to the underlying meanings she attributed and the surprises she concocted along the way. Her details certainly sprinkled unceasing magic.

*My mother with our dear Millie riding a bicycle on Bayshore Boulevard, in front of "La Rubia."*

CHAPTER SIX

# No Ordinary Day

*Don't worry, be happy.*

MAY 13, 2013

When Ana Young is your mother, no day is ordinary. Simple tasks like shopping at the grocery store become social gatherings resembling family reunions with long lost relatives, or in this case store clerks.

"Oh, how she's grown!" remarks Sunny at the Commissary at MacDill Air Force Base, befriended since I was five.

Like all family reunions however, the topics discussed between adults carry little to no interest for a child, so I usually spent my time daydreaming about the Dunkaroos I hoped we'd pick up in aisle 10. But Ana would continue her captivating conversation, and pretty soon, a whole flock of "relatives" emerged to join in on the fun. I remember questioning whether my mom was a celebrity. Turns out, she was far more well-known.

Everywhere we went was like a long-anticipated reunion. Nordstrom was never just a place to buy clothes. It was a time to disclose future travels with Joann or reminisce about passed love ones with Bradley. My mother won the hearts of everyone she met, whether at the Commissary or Publix, Walgreens or Carrabba's.

"She's so cute!" commented every sales associate or representative when my mother wasn't paying attention. My sister and I, accustomed to this claim, nodded in agreement, and inevitably witnessed disclosure of new discounts, exceptions to expired coupons, and the fostering of new friendships unfold before our eyes.

    The number of times I've used the phrase, "I'm Ana Young's daughter" is too numerous to count. However, no matter how many times I have articulated those words, I continue to feel this intense pride emanating from each sound and syllable. Me, the daughter of Ana M. Young, one of humanity's finest creatures, one of intellect's most astute students, one of God's most faithful servants. Ana Young. Not just the miracle maker, the walking miracle herself.

    Every day becomes this miracle to be alive. Nothing happens just to happen. Rather, each action, word, complication, success occurs for a reason, a reason sometimes so obscure and questionable in the present moment, but a reason, nonetheless.

    Ana believed in the following truth: reasons for why things happen emerge through a clarity procured with time and faith.

    One day in particular highlights this very concept. The year of my college graduation, I decided to run the fortieth Annual Chicago Marathon for the American Cancer Society in honor of my beautiful Queen and grandfather, who, as mentioned previously, battled tongue cancer for the last eighteen years of his life.

    The day after my race, my family and I were driving a rental car to Chicago O'Hare Airport to take our flight back to Tampa. Halfway through the trip, a car suddenly and violently rear-ends us, so intensely, that our vehicle is barely able to pull over to the side of the road. Thankfully, no one was hurt in the accident, but we still had to call the police and file a report. After about an hour, the police finally show up and my dad gets out of the car to handle the situation.

    Now the cop, a Chicago native, is acting as though the Cubs did not just win the World Series the previous year.

    "Sir, I'm going to have to ask you to shut the f*** up," responds the police officer to my taken-aback father.

    Not wanting to aggravate the situation further and knowing that

Officer Smith is just doing his job, my dad steps aside and proceeds to talk only when necessary.

"So, was there anyone else with ya in the car?" the officer questions.

"Yes, my family is actually waiting in the car" my dad responds.

"Wait here," he says.

Without probing any further, the officer walks over to the car, and begins the standard protocol of interrogation. But with Ana Young smiling in the front seat with her perfect hair, pearls, and pearly whites, we would not have guessed in our wildest imagination that this policeman had ever been rude to my father. The conversation was so pleasant, that we were at the point of wanting to offer this man donuts and coffee. About ten minutes go by, and our new constable friend finally departs.

In a completely different demeanor, the officer exclaims to dad, "Your family is awesome!! I just spoke with them and they are so lovely. Do you want us to escort you to the airport so you can make your flight in time?"

Ana Young was able to change the man's countenance from dreary to dreamy in a matter of minutes. That was also the day I rode in the backseat of a cop car, without the encumbrance of having to commit a crime. Again, another twenty-four hours that were anything but ordinary.

Now, I can't say for sure why this specific event transpired. However, what I do know is God probably saved us from something more serious, beyond the hassle and stress that comes with automobile accidents. He also probably saved someone else from a perhaps deadly collision with the drunken offender. Who knows, maybe even the officer needed an interaction with Ana Young to brighten his day and alter his perspective for good. God works in mysterious ways, a truth my mother held dear, supplementing her optimism and ability to extract goodness out of every situation.

Another example of transforming normal to remarkable comes from a class project for my geography class in the fourth grade. Tasked with compiling information about a country of Ms. Teddar's choosing, I disclosed the assignment to my esteemed confidante, the magnificent Ana Young. Without hesitation, she suggested I turn a simple book report into a three-dimensional demonstration of the country's growth per capita. Part of the vision involved procuring flags of said country, and she knew just the place.

The next day, we drove to a quaint shop around the corner from my favorite ice cream parlor. An older man welcomed us into his store, which was filled with an impressive number of flags, large and small, from all over the world. I can only imagine what this man did on June 14th.

In a classic response to Ana Young, the storekeeper became enamored with my beautiful mother's intrinsic curiosity with the world. In addition to asking the basic questions heard from most customers such as, "Do you have Gambia's flag," my mother layered in her advanced intellect by further probing, "Did you hear the news about Gambia's new government?"

The conversation continued to escalate. Pretty soon, we were addressing existential quandaries regarding life's meaning.

"The most important word in life is initiative," the man articulated. "The root of success comes back to having the initiative to go after things in life."

This resonated greatly with Valedictorian Ana Young, and thus we spent the next hour lauding the word *initiative* for everything it stood for. Personal anecdotes abounded as the word kept sinking deeper into my long-term memory.

And so, I had been Ana Young'd again. A regular day spent preparing for a class project became the backdrop to a profound discussion on the essence of life, not to mention an expansion to my fourth-grade vocabulary.

Growing up, errands such as the flag acquisition sometimes led to humorous memories. For example, one time my mother wanted to get her shoe fixed by our local cobbler (Apparently, this was a common occurrence, but this time there were no holiday breads involved).

It was supposed to be a quick task, since my mother had to simply drop off the damaged footwear for the cobbler to fix. So, she left me and my sister in the car for a couple of minutes. Having always raised us to be aware of our surroundings, upon witnessing a rather large man with an unwelcoming look approach the shop, I did what my mother taught me to do: I hid.

As the more cautious of the two, I begged my sister to do the same, yelling "duck" to signal the warning that an attack was imminent should the man see us. I realize now just how nonsensical this line of thinking was and why my older sister did not follow suit, especially considering the man was nowhere near the car and was clearly headed to the store since he too sported a dilapidated shoe. At the time, however, my mother's instruction to always exaggerate when it came to our safety echoed in my mind, so I army-crawled into the back seat of our Ford Expedition. As my sister looked onward in the front seat, my curiosity peaked because her facial expression darkened. Apparently, my mother, upon turning to leave the store, saw the man and in a frightful upwards gaze, stood paralyzed. By the time I popped my head up to see what was going on, my mother was nowhere in sight, blocked by the giant man like a wide receiver making a play against the defensive lineman. Her face pale and her fear conspicuous, for she instantaneously reappeared, darting left and right to seemingly evade the man and return to her daughters. Pretty soon, she jumped in the car and took off so fast, you would have thought she robbed the store.

Yes, was this an exaggeration? Absolutely. Was the large man an innocent bystander? No doubt in my mind. But if it came to our safety, my mother stopped at nothing to ensure we were so far removed from danger that the word would never cross our minds.

Except, of course, if there were cockroaches involved.

One day, after having picked us up from school, my mother did as she normally did: she pulled the car up to our neighborhood mailbox on the other end of the block to collect the mail before heading home. Once the mail was secured, she returned to the car, set the piles of magazines and envelopes on her lap, and continued to drive towards our house.

Suddenly, my mother jumps out of the moving vehicle and the papers go flying into the street like a frazzled Peter Pan and Wendy. Not understanding what was happening, I turn to my sister with a confused look for the inexplicable event that just occurred.

At the time, I didn't really understand how cars worked, nor did I know how to operate such machinery. So, I was confused how we were still moving without a driver. Glancing forward, as our closed garage door crept closer than ever before, my mother in the nick of time jumped back into the car and hit the brakes. We were saved.

After the panic settled and the sense of an impending collision subsided, we proceeded to ask My Queen what in the world caused her to jump out of a moving vehicle. Turns out, there was a large cockroach in the ruffles of the mail, so she reacted in the best way she knew how: she fled. What fled as well were the copious pieces of paper mail drifting throughout the block. However, once we collected ourselves and the remnants of our post, uncontrollable laughter ensued.

My mother was a serious lady. She was a responsible individual who understood the value of propriety and always carried herself with an air of dignity. But when life threw laughable moments at her, she knew how to bask in the hilarity of it all. She loved to laugh, to smile, and to enjoy these comical moments of life.

It took me a few days to restore my inner peace as an afterschool passenger, but at least no more cockroaches were ever spotted inside my mother's post.

Trips to Disney… now those words alone certainly imply the transcendence of *ordinary*. Add Ana Young to the mix, and you encounter magic far beyond the caliber of pixie dust.

To add pizzazz to our Disney adventures, my beautiful mother always wore a themed hat, shirt, jacket, or dress, purchased at one of Disney's awe-inspiring bazars. We used to leave the Wonderful World of Disney store having fallen prey to the glamour of overpriced merchandise. Bags full, hearts ready, and financial anxiety on the horizon. Regardless of these budgetary constraints, my beautiful mother was perpetually draped in Disney perfection… and never without her pearls.

As aforementioned, every year for my birthday, we would venture to the land of the mouse. And 2017 was no different. In fact, that year, we were fulfilling another lifelong dream of mine: spending the night at The Grand Floridian after gallivanting about in the Magic Kingdom for Mickey's Very Merry Christmas Party.

And so, after work that Friday, the four of us hopped in our Escalade, and started down I-4 towards what I thought would be a nice break from all the present-day stress.

Upon arriving at the hotel, my heart sang. The place smelled of peppermint and paradise, as we passed the beautifully adorned entryway and laid our eyes on the life-size gingerbread house in the corner. And you better believe my eyes glimmered at the magnificence of the Christmas tree that stood in the middle of the grand lobby. To top it all off, Mickey and Minnie were taking photos with guests in front of my dream tree. I immediately felt drawn to participate in the photographic activity.

After having checked in, we approached the crowd and joined the line, daydreaming about the magic that was soon to be had.

After about twenty minutes of waiting, our turn had finally arrived.

Now this next part is all a blur, in part due to the sheer excitement of reuniting with my old pals Mickey and Minnie, but also due to the atypical series of events that took place. After a few moments of assembling, just as we were about to have our picture taken, my mother instantly panics.

"Where's my watch?!" she exclaims to the bewildered photographer.

Her Rolex was missing.

Now, my beautiful mother, because of her intellectual prowess, perfectionistic nature, and motherly instinct, tended to worry, sometimes drawing conclusions prior to fully understanding the complete context of a situation. So next thing we knew, my mother starts accusing Mickey and Minnie of stealing one of her most prized possessions.

I thought to myself, how would that even be possible? For one, I doubted they would try and pull off such a stunt in front of large groups of children, inevitably stripping away their innocence faster than you can say "heartburn medication." But also, it was highly unlikely because the characters lacked fully functioning fingers. Thus, stealthy pickpocketing was far from probable. Yet, there we were, with whatever was left of my childhood withering away before my very eyes, along with the inner lining of my esophagus.

In an instant, my mother and sister stepped away. I, not knowing what to do, posed for a quick photo with Mr. & Mrs. Mouse as my mother scurried off to speak with the manager.

Now, at the time, it was an absolute travesty to have lost the Rolex, a dream she had not been able to realize until recently on our trip to Paris. However, once we discovered the truth about the watch, that my mother had left it at our house in Tampa (a fact ascertained by my father driving back and forth that very night), my beautiful Queen had won the heart and soul of the hotel manager. So strong was the new bond between the two that he not only upgraded our room, but he also granted us a free character breakfast the following morning.

So what was a stressful situation became an exhilarating display of Ana Young magic, resulting in an even better conviviality in our home away from home.

Not an ordinary day indeed.

Even the circumstances of obtaining the famous watch lack "ordinary" in their description. That trip to Paris was something out of a fairytale.

Stemming from my desire to attain fluency in the French language, a yearning inspired by the example of both my mother and grandfather, I decided to sign up for a French Immersion Program at the American University of Paris (AUP) during the summer after my freshman year at Notre Dame. Rather than sending me to Europe alone, my beautiful Queen decided to tag along with my sister and make it a "girls trip."

To thwart any potential danger or risk that could accompany apartment living in a foreign country, my beautiful Queen decides that the three of us will stay in Hôtel Du Louvre during the entirety of my program. This majestic, ideally located hotel became our home for a surreal four weeks. I kid you not when I say that every moment of Mom's magic had culminated in this very trip. The "Ana Young Effect" had reached its apex.

In our new Parisian home, we were treated like *Downton Abbey* royalty. Well, my mother and sister more so than me. I was the random girl who would show up on occasion when I was not studying or in class.

For those who have never watched the show, *Downton Abbey* is about an aristocratic family in twentieth century England who, because of their noble title, live in a stunning castle with maids, butlers, footmen, chauffeurs, and chefs who wait on them hand and foot. This is how it felt during our stay. We became the Grantham family in modern day France. Those at the front desk, the concierge, the bellboys, and waiters… everyone knew and adored My Queen.

The adventures we had all started on the first day.

As part of orientation, the newly enrolled students at AUP were going to be taken on a boat tour down the Seine, in craft called *bateaux-mouches*. Not knowing the exact address or location of the return embarkment (in addition to not being able to pronounce the words) my mother began to panic for my safety. Without viable cellular service, knowledge of the city, or proficiency in the language, my concerned mother decided to try her luck with the hotel staff's telepathic abilities to see if they could perhaps shed some light. So, with the orientation schedule in hand, she pleaded for an hour with the concierge to understand where her daughter was being taken.

 Because Paris is an international city, most people understood English. And so, throughout the entire trip, my mother spoke the language of her American home. However, for some reason, whenever a word containing the letter "r" would arise, she became a regular Jacques Clouseau in the middle of her sentence.

 "Please Pierre, I'm so 'so**rr**y' but I'm trying not to 'wo**rr**y,'" she pleaded, isolating the words "sorry" and "worry" in her new phlegm-like fashion.

 But there was only so much poor Pierre could do with such limited information. To this day, I'm not entirely sure how they found me. Thanks to Pierre and his patience, as soon as I disembarked the *bateau-mouche*, there they were, waiting for me vigilantly. Not knowing the extent of apprehension, I was perplexed why my mother hugged me as if I had come back from D-Day in Normandy. Regardless, I was just happy to be home in her embrace yet again.

 My beautiful mother's concern did not stop at boat rides. Because of the "dangers" of public transport for a young female of nineteen, my mother decided to drop me off at my university every day. And so, every morning, the three of us would hop in a cab, my mother and sister would drop me off at school and pick me up after class. Every day, after having spent an intense four hours in French-speaking bootcamp, I was completely exhausted. The last possible thing I wanted to do was articulate a single word in any language, but especially in French. And without fail, despite several pleas, the first thing my mother would do was start conversing with the cab driver in her broken "r" letter *Frenglish*, glaring at me with a sharp stare that suggested I was obliged to continue the conversation.

For context, during this time, ISIS terrorist attacks were a prevalent threat in the world, a reality that scared my beautiful mother to no end. For years, even beyond this trip, her fear guided her down the path of suspecting anyone and everyone as an associate of this extremist group. Everyone was potentially from ISIS: hospital workers, postal service employees, random plane passengers... no one could be discredited. Even at the hotel, at the onset of our stay, she feared one of the bellboys, Philippe, an older man whom my mother suspected due to his constant questioning, or how someone else might interpret it, affable demeanor. Every time we would leave our hotel room, if we caught sight of poor Philippe, Mom would signal as if we were in the most precarious of situations to dash out of harm's way. Next thing I knew we were sneaking across the halls as though participating in some laser tag tournament against the elderly. Thankfully, the fear inevitably subsided, but only after our Q-ZAR adversary delivered free macarons and champagne to our room one evening.

After that, my mother purposefully sought Phillipe's presence in our lives, continuously expressing thoughts throughout the day like "Oh I have to share this later with Phillippe!" and "Oh I wonder where Phillippe is?" and "I hope we run into Philippe!" An interesting turn of events to say the least.

Naturally, her worry for the unknown and fear of the ISIS extremist group led her to take caution against our cab drivers.

"Our fate rests in their hands," my mother rationalized her suspicion.

Her tactic in ensuring our safety inside the taxi? Become friends with the driver through conversation to circumvent any possible threats.

"I'm 'so**rr**y,' sir, but we are in a 'hu**rr**y,'" she'd start, with her full-fledged "**r**" letter phlegm-like language.

*"Pas un problème,"* the driver responded. (Translation: Not to worry).

Cue the intimidating look, and there I was, spending an additional twenty minutes of my French immersion practices, without any extra credit. So rather than enjoying a peaceful sojourn throughout the beautiful city, I endured mental duress during what became stressful survival experiences.

I think the most disquieting situation of our Parisian adventure was our day trip to visit Monet's gardens in Giverny, a city about an hour or so in the outskirts of Paris. Our tour guide and driver seemed normal and friendly when we first met him at the hotel. But once he was behind the wheel, the man was a complete nutcase. He started cursing in French, breaking every traffic rule within seconds (usually not very hard to do in Paris, since there are so few; but even for Paris, it was alarming), and "shooting" with a fake gun formed by his hand at those who "crossed his path" **four lanes over.**

Usually, when my mom is concerned, there is a chance that she's overly cautious again about, let's say Marty, a salesperson at our local Home Depot and his potential hidden agenda. This time, however, my sister and I can validate her trepidation. I could see the panic in her eyes as this dangerous man transported us throughout the day.

Thankfully, nothing happened on our tour, and Monet's gardens turned out to be even more beautiful than his paintings. But that did not stop my mother from taking just another precautionary measure. At the end of the day, she insisted we take a group photo with the two other families and the tour guide, just to have photographic evidence of this madman should he prove dangerous in the future. Honestly, a very good idea against Paris's Street's Most Wanted.

And so, after the adventure and the makings of a very poor Yelp review, we ate the most delicious German meal at La Brasserie Lipp, and headed home in the hopes of sharing the day's happenings with Philippe.

On most mornings during our Parisian adventure, we would partake in the delicious buffet-style breakfast, fit for Anglican noblesse. On the mornings we struggled to wake up in time, only my mother and sister would indulge as they returned to the hotel after dropping me off at my university. One of the waiters, a young Chilean man, thus grew accustomed to seeing my mother and sister dine at his restaurant, and before I knew it, another friendship emerged. My sister and I however were convinced that the twenty-seven-year-old Chilean was in love with our beautiful mother, which only added to the fun. But honestly, who wasn't in love with my mother is the better question.

So, while my sister and mother enjoyed their delicious breakfast after having taken a stroll through the exquisite city of Paris, I painstakingly watched the clock until our first break, involving a much-needed *pain au chocolat* and coffee. Regardless of the extra rest and the other adventures I missed out on due to class, such as lunches in front of the Eiffel Tower, it was always the best feeling to come home to my sister and the arms of my beautiful Queen.

One of the most memorable days was the day we were going to head to Champagne, France to visit the birthplace of my favorite bubbly beverage. However, it was the most joyous not because of the actual trip, but because when our alarms went off at three o'clock that morning, we unanimously decided to forgo the trip and go back to sleep. Despite not recuperating lost funds and missing out on a once-in-a-lifetime experience, I can honestly say with the utmost sincerity that I will never forget the all-consuming joy of falling back asleep that morning. It was the purest of bliss, dream-like if you will.

That was the beauty about Ana Young. Even something as humdrum as falling back asleep would transform into a remarkable memory.

As if our trip could not seem more surreal, there were a few days when my cousin, aunt, and grandmother were also in Paris at the same time we were. This led to more adventures including racing in man-powered-carts to arrive at our restaurant, Le Relais de l'Entrecôte, partying the night away at Buddha-Bar with Jordi, our cousin, ending up inside one of the fountains of Place de la Concorde and a rough trip to Versailles the next morning, dancing in front of the pyramid right next to the Louvre Museum as Paris scintillated at night, and of course celebrating my sister's twenty-first birthday at the restaurant inside the Eiffel Tower, to name a few. They certainly added to the unforgettable nature of the trip.

    As previously mentioned, on this trip, my mother accomplished a lifelong dream of purchasing her very own Rolex watch, an accessory worn and cherished by my grandfather for many years. Thus, my mother had always dreamt of having one of her very own. I remember the tangible joy she experienced when we made it a reality.

    Another dream of hers was taking us to hear the *Requiem de Mozart* in the historic and magnificent church, La Madeleine, in the heart of Paris. The powerful piece of music reverberated the breathtaking antiquated structures, and my mother beaming all the while. It truly was surreal.

    Another dreamlike experience that turned an ordinary day into an extraordinary one was the fact that one of my best friends from college, Faye Zhou, was also passing through Paris on her European summer vacation. Not only was it so fun to see her for a few days, but also Faye provided us with the idea of attending the French Open, the annual tennis tournament that happened to be taking place at the same time we were in Paris. And so, there we went, the four of us dressed to the nines to witness the spectacle of Roland Garros.

    After my French Immersion Program ended, we spent a few days in Amsterdam and Belgium, traveling there by train. I will never forget the picturesque canals, the unimaginable conditions of Anne Frank's house, the illustrious works of Rembrandt at the Rijksmuseum, the different levels and layers of activity at the Heineken Experience, and the unprecedented number of bicycles in Amsterdam. In Belgium, besides the incredible architecture, beautiful works of lace, stately tapestries, divine waffles, and magnificent mayonnaise-infused fries, the pinnacle of my experience was entering the first Godiva store, located in the corner of Brussels's main square, with the streets leading up to it laden with chocolate shops large and small. I knew I was finally where I belonged.

My mother would later recount that one of her favorite parts of the entire trip was the fact that I was so overcome with emotion from being in the historic setting of my favorite chocolate brand, that I even cried. Yes, there I was, like a kid in a candy store, crying tears of joy in the place of conception of the most spectacular cocoa confection.

Upon returning to Paris, we knew exactly where we wanted to spend our last meal. Throughout our stay in the "City of Lights," our favorite restaurant was right across the street from the hotel on the corner of l'Avenue de l'Opéra, where the three of us would always order spaghetti while sitting outside on the bustling Parisian street. On our final night, Paris was even more vibrant than usual; music and sounds filled the streets and arrondissements. Turns out it was the Fête de la Musique, their annual celebration of music on the day of the summer solstice. It felt as though Paris was saying goodbye in a sweet-sounding expression of symphonic singularity. And I'd be remiss if I didn't say it *struck a chord* with us.

And so, as our trip to Paris came to a close, and the *Downton Abbey* experience lasting only one more night, the staff, so enamored by my beautiful mother, surprised us with a free stay in the hotel's master suite.

"How can I 'ever' 'repay' you?" The Queen humbly inquired, with her French-like pronounced rs.

"The pleasure was ours," Hotel Du Louvre's manager responded.

Now I wish I could say we spent our last night relaxing in our new, awe-inspiringly beautiful hotel room, reminiscing about all the wonderful experiences of our time in Paris. Unfortunately, this was not the case.

At first, entering the room and marveling at the spectacle before us took about twenty minutes to fully grasp the idea that we were worthy of spending the night there (well my sister and I, my mom obviously was more than worthy). But after the novelty faded, and the afternoon started slowly slipping away, my sister started developing symptoms that would indicate something was clearly wrong with her stomach. And so, as my mom catered to her needs, and my sister struggled to function, I was left alone to solve the world's most difficult Tetris problem: three suitcases, three women, four weeks in Paris… how in the world was it all going to fit. Usually when I travel, I strategically pack items in a way that will circumvent the fifty-pound weight limitation for luggage on all flights, foreign and domestic. Not that night. For the first time in my life, overweight fees were a non-issue in my mind. I was shoving scarves and shoes in every nook and cranny of the three-part modern-day enigma machine. And yet, contrary to the laws of physics and femininity, I cracked the quandary and managed to not only finish packing, but also straightened out all the paperwork needed for the following day.

As always, the morning came too quickly. And with tears in our eyes, we said our goodbyes, and bid our "summer" home adieu.

Jean Luc, our driver from the first day, had an uncanny resemblance to my uncle Tío Joey. This fact provided a sense of comfort, especially when looking back upon previous cab drivers and tour guides. Thankfully, he had come back to take us to the airport.

My sister, still ill, and my mother, still concerned for her wellbeing, left me alone in a foreign airport to deal with the VAT refund and overweight luggage. Sensing my need for help, Jean Luc stepped in like a godsent messiah, something Americans rarely say about the French. He offered to push one of our luggage carts and proceeded to explain the process of collecting our tax refund. I have never loved a stranger more than my Parisian uncle.

And so, after much hullabaloo, a hefty luggage fee, and bypassing a bomb threat in the middle of the airport, we arrived at our gate, and flew home.

I will never forget that summer so infused with the spirit of Ana Young.

A year later, I decided to further expand my cultural horizons by applying for Notre Dame's London Summer Abroad program. My mother loved England and thus would look for any excuse to travel back to the "motherland." Once I was accepted to the program, she knew she had to capitalize on the opportunity.

And so, after my six-week program ended, my mother came to "pick me up" with my grandmother, during which we spent seven glorious days basking in bustling London town. Because my mother and grandmother had already been to London on several different occasions, and I had already spent six magnificent weeks discovering all its wonders, we did not feel obliged to partake in the usual tourist activities. Rather, we spent the week relaxing, enjoying each other's company, and reaping the benefits of our wonderful hotel, The Rubens, located across the street from Buckingham Palace. Another surreal experience, our daily routine was of course, fit for a queen: wake up at 9 a.m., have breakfast at 9:30 a.m., go back to the room to take a nap, take a leisurely stroll to the Queen's shop around the corner, spend roughly two hours purchasing and marveling at beautiful pieces of china, walk back to the hotel for tea time during which we'd spectate passersby, hoping to catch a glimpse of one of the members of the royal family, consume chicken with curry for dinner, and finish the day enjoying a movie in our room. Again, who has or seeks these experiences but Ana Young?

Once the rest of the family arrived in London, we set sail on a cruise that took us around the British Isles. My sister and I were the youngest on board by twenty years, but that did not stop us from relishing in the joys of our seafaring adventure.

Come nightfall, you'd expect my sister to be the one more inclined to boogie on the dance floor. Come to think of it, perhaps she didn't because I used such terminology in my request. Regardless, my beautiful Queen, the one and only Ana Young, found herself along for the groovy ride (if you're shaking your head in disappointment, you wouldn't be the first). Everyone else would just gaze as the dynamic mother-daughter duo shredded the dance floor. As the night progressed, some people even joined! Most, however, were too old, so they were down for the count by seven. Regardless of who participated, I was thriving rhythmically alongside My Queen.

The dancing didn't end there. It was further heightened when the cruise took us to Liverpool. My uncles were extremely hesitant about visiting the token Beatles attractions, claiming them to be "tourist traps." But my thought was, what else does one do in Liverpool if not cross Abbey Road or visit Penny Lane and John Lennon's house? After a few moments of debate, they conceded and we made our way to the land of English music nobility.

Our first stop was a bit of a drive, so most of us fell asleep. But as soon as we entered the city, our tour guide, a fellow Beatles enthusiast, started blasting "Love Me Do," as an alarm clock, and you better believe my mother and I started dancing just as we had done the night before. I'll never forget how happy we were in that moment, entering the land of my ancestors (my great grandfather on my father's side was from Liverpool), with my beautiful Queen, who in that moment would have knighted the Beatles herself.

Another one of our stops was in Belfast, Northern Ireland. This city is famous for being the city where the Titanic was manufactured. Thus, we visited the Titanic Museum as part of the day's itinerary. My beautiful mother, because of her natural optimism and love of gift shops, purchased countless objects with the Titanic logo and name splattered across every scarf, sock, purse, and pen she purchased. Later that evening, however, I woke up to find my mother wide awake, looking out across the great span of darkness from our cruise room window. There was a great deal of fog, so the captain kept blasting the horn throughout the night. Because it was two in the morning, most of us did not wake up to the sound of the crew's advisory, except for my mother.

"Es que Cath, how could we go to the museum of a ship that sank when we ourselves are on a ship! I couldn't sleep because of it and now this fog… " she articulated with a bit of panic in her voice.

I couldn't help but hug and console her. After imparting a few words of wisdom and waking up a bit more with each horn blast, I looked to my right and saw one of the Titanic branded purses my mother purchased. I immediately saw the humor in it and started uncontrollably laughing.

In between breaths, I explained, "Mom do you realize how ironic it is that you bought so many things from the Titanic store to wear and use on a cruise?"

We immediately burst into laughter, transforming the worry into comedic relief.

Two very unforgettable summers indeed.

I could go on, pointing out the several other voyages we embarked on and the unforgettable memories that highlight the daily transcendence of ordinary with Ana Young. But unfortunately, there aren't enough trees to supply the pages it would take to capture them all. So for now, these will have to *(Love Me)* do.

*My beautiful mother and I after  
I ran the 2017 Chicago Marathon  
in her honor.*

## CHAPTER SEVEN

# A Life to Stomach

*If you suffer with meaning, it's different.*

**FEBRUARY 13, 2019**

When Ana Young is your mother, you begin to develop a profound admiration for food from day one, lending yourself to exotic meals at a very young age just to follow her example.

"I'll have the duck à l'orange please," I said in my eight-year-old wisdom, catching a glimpse of my beautiful mother as we both enjoyed our salads drenched in blue cheese.

You can imagine the disappointment of my father for not having ordered off the kids' menu as he received the bill.

"In life, you don't have to suffer," these were the words often heard by me and my sister when aches or complaints inevitably arose.

My beautiful mother believed in the following truth: you can either be a victim of life or a "doer." As a nine-year-old, I didn't quite capture this profound statement when faced with a headache but learned to understand her words when she reached for the Tylenol.

Life is about choices. You can either sit there and sulk and do nothing. Or you can face the problem head-on and take the Tylenol.

How does this relate to food? I'll explain.

My beautiful mother decided one day when she was little that she would like everything because she knew it would make her life easier and prevent future "suffering."

"Eat everything, and life will be easier," she'd state as my four-year-old self stared unenthusiastically at the Guatemalan frijoles, whose appearance somewhat resembled human waste.

But as the time passed, and trips to Guatemala and Europe accumulated, I now can proudly say I eat anything and everything...and life is easier. I never had to worry I'd starve at a sleepover or birthday party because I could always eat the food provided. I never have to disappoint family members or friends who try out new recipes because chances are, I will love the dish. I will always enjoy my days reveling in the consumption of whatever life throws at me, preventing the headaches and Tylenol all together.

One of my favorite representations of this belief comes from when my beautiful mother volunteered to provide lunch one day for my sister's kindergarten class. Rather than conceding to the standard cuisine of infantile children, my mother ordered Blimpie Bests with *everything* on them for every four-year-old in Mrs. Buyer's class. Banana peppers, green peppers, jalapeño peppers, onions, olives, literally every topping available filled each sandwich to the brink of hand cramping capacity. Concerned for the class's unrefined palate, my father asked my mother if she was sure this was a good idea.

"They need to learn to like everything," Ana crisply responded, ignoring the children's grimacing faces as they met their match in BLT bemusement.

And so, by refusing to order the standard Chick-fil-A party platter for the class, my mother in her infinite wisdom, strived to make this lesson of refining one's palate for the procurement of an easier life widely known at the onset of childhood. Now I'm not sure Mrs. Buyer's class captured this lesson when unwillingly facing the banana peppers, but at least they were given the opportunity to try.

When Ana Young is your mother, you share her appreciation for not only the delicacy of each cuisine, but also the belief that food is a gift, a gateway to cultures, an introduction to lifestyles. By trying everything, you engage in the opportunity to learn something new about a foreign land. Your travels are enhanced, and your palate expanded. Your heart, always ready to discover, and your stomach, more than willing to partake.

Such a mentality is the reason why we did not feel squeamish to try the dish *black pudding* when in London for the first time. For those of you who don't know, black pudding is made from pork blood, with pork or beef fat mixed with oats. However sanguinary the treat, we stopped at nothing if it meant cultural discovery.

This mindset paired with the optimism of Ana Young truly made our travels abroad that much more enriching.

One of the most memorable trips we took, primarily due to the endless buffet open twenty-four hours a day, was a family cruise around the Mediterranean to celebrate my grandfather's eightieth birthday. Twenty family members on one ship certainly constituted a party.

I remember feeling so excited about spending two whole weeks with my fellow cousins. Naturally this led to many adventures, most of which occurred on the opposite side of the ship from where all the adults were staying.

To streamline communication aboard the colossal cruise ship, many family members acceded to utilizing walkie-talkies.

"Mocha, Mocha, this is Skittles… over," my cousin Felipe articulated through his handheld transmitter to signal for my attention.

Feeling like a secret agent in a Jason Bourne movie with our stealthy, food-inspired code names, I responded, "Skittles, Skittles this is Mocha, what's your location… over."

We were so excited and intense about using such clandestine tactics, you might have thought our subsequent activities involved saving all cruise ship passengers from an impending iceberg; the reality is we just wanted to know if the other wanted to grab free ice cream near the front of the ship.

Apparently, our older cousins did not take as much of a liking to hearing our continuous exchanges, forcing us to use a different radio frequency altogether. Regardless, the walkie-talkies were a lifesaver in the pre-cellphone era, and the ice cream was well worth the trouble.

Aside from our dabbles in espionage communication, the most movie-like occurrence to take place on this vacation materialized during our stop in the Grecian Island of Mykonos. One of the most spectacular places I have ever visited, Mykonos will always hold a special memory in my mind for reasons beyond the clear-blue water and picturesque architecture.

As part of the day's excursions, the family decided to rent scooters to explore the magnificent sights of this scenic city. There were not enough scooters to go around, so most of my family members had to pair up. As one of the youngest cousins, I of course chose to pair with my beautiful Queen. However, as an exceptionally cautious woman, my mother decides at the last second that she did not feel comfortable operating the unfamiliar piece of Greek machinery, worrying she would put my life in danger. As a result, the others left to tour the island and I stayed behind wondering just what was behind those beautiful rolling hills.

About twenty minutes go by, and I see half of the group is back, including my father who had taken my sister on the initial trek. My father, feeling guilty that I was the only cousin left behind offered to take me through a quick stroll with six other family members who wanted to visit a little church where my aunt and uncle renewed their wedding vows five years prior.

Once I received the reluctant nod of approval from my sweet mother, I hopped on the Vespa, and off we went. I remember looking upon the hills and thinking to myself just how glorious it felt to be alive.

And then those thoughts came to a crashing halt.

After having visited the church, the group decided it was time to go back. As we turned around, the scooter my father and I were riding decided to give up faster than a pastry chef on a diet.

The other family members noticed our troubles and immediately took off to seek help. The issue wasn't the fact that we could not get back. The problem was time.

Every day, passengers had to be back on the cruise ship by 5 p.m. to allow sufficient time to sail to our next destination. If one wasn't back, the cruise would leave. No exceptions.

It was 4 p.m.

Everything happened so fast. The seconds and minutes all slipped by as my father and I kept trying to kickstart the scooter by manually pushing the machine, but to no avail. As we continued our fruitless efforts, we found, perched on top of one of the hills, a dilapidated hut that resembled the workings of a local gas station.

4:30 p.m. hit, and so did my panic.

As my father attempted to converse with an older man who appeared to work there, I began feeling petrified at the thought of being separated from the rest of my family, but mostly being stranded in a foreign country without my passport, and without my mom.

As soon as my father came back, the adrenaline swiftly pushed those thoughts to the back of my brain. We continued to push and ride, push and ride. Suddenly, a fast-approaching Jeep violently swerved in front of us. I was so relieved to see the hairy, Greek man from the scooter shop and my cousin Jordi. He hopped out of the car, and said, "Get in."

It was 4:48 p.m.

Without questioning, we did as we were told. The four of us flew back to the shop in a turbulent frenzy. Upon arrival, we found my mother bawling her eyes out due to the potential separation. The next part is all a blur, but I remember hearing the *Chariots of Fire* theme song in the background as my mother, father, sister, aunt, uncle, cousins, and I sprinted towards the ship as if in a slow-motion scene of an action-packed film. Pan to the ship, and the rest of the passengers cheered us on as we victoriously made it just before the clock struck five.

Apparently back on the cruise, a few of my family members had no idea we were missing until the Captain made several announcements over the cruise-wide intercom, inquiring about our whereabouts like vagabond criminals, guilty of unacceptable tardiness. Our photos were even flashed on every television on board.

Needless to say, I never again questioned My Queen's instincts regarding foreign transportation.

Another quasi-cinematic experience happened on the day at sea after the tumultuous Mykonos visit. Felipe, aka "Skittles," Martín, our youngest cousin, my sister, and I were all spending time together after a glorious visit to the cruise buffet. Near the front of the ship, my sister and Martín were racing each other along the side. As the races continued, Felipe and I conversed sans walkie-talkie, but noticed that Margaret Anne and Martín had taken longer than usual to return. Not thinking anything of it, we started making our way along the side of the ship but did not find them on our path. The more we pressed on, the stronger the wind became, suppressing our ability to walk upright altogether. At one point, the gusts were so powerful, we found ourselves holding onto the handrail for dear life.

I started shouting, "Margaret Anne! Where are you?!"

Nothing. My voice lost by the overpowering gale. We pressed on, clenching the railing as if our lives depended on it.

By the time we reached the front of the ship, we were crawling on the floor, like an out-of-shape weatherman hunting hurricanes for live coverage. After a few more arduous steps, we found them. My sister, on top of Martín to prevent his seventy-pound body from blowing away, was crouched down, eyes closed, and holding onto dear life.

"We have to keep going," I shouted.

"What?!" My sister replied, not being able to make out my words due to the deafening howl.

"We have to keep going!" I repeated, making a signal to help our line of communication.

She nodded, I looked behind and noticed Felipe looked like he was almost going to blow away as well. I knew we had to get out of there.

I gave him the signal, and off we went, with great difficulty and a tremendous amount of fear. Thankfully, we made it to the other side and the wind eventually subsided, along with any prospects of a future career in weather reporting.

I can't even imagine what we must have looked like, not only because of our windswept hair and frightened demeanor, but to those working out inside the cruise's gym, which was directly behind the glass window that separated us from the inside of the ship. Later that day, we came to learn that our older cousin, María Olga, had a front-row seat of our escapade while on the elliptical.

"Are you guys ok?"

"Define ok," I said to myself, referring mostly to the PTSD I felt when a gust of the ship's air conditioning blew on my face as she asked a few hours later.

We laugh about it now, but honestly, I can confirm Jack and Rose's experience at the front of the ship was very different than mine. I am *blown away* by that fact.

Apparently, news of our windswept adventure did not make its way to my father and grandfather. That night after dinner, despite being told not to go outside by my grandmother and mother, they made the same mistake of nearing the front of the ship. Only this time, they did it without the solace of light. My father recounts that experience with a gratitude to God for not having lost Don Rafael to the sea. Imagine, my grandfather, whose birthday we were celebrating, an eighty-year-old man who required a walking stick experiencing the same hurricane-like winds in an ill-lit environment. Not even Ernest Hemingway could have fathomed such a premise.

Otherwise, that trip was a compilation of great memories such as traveling to Spain, Turkey, Greece, Italy, and even Lourdes, France to visit the original Grotto where the Virgin Mary appeared to Saint Bernadette. One of the most awe-inspiring experiences of my life, Lourdes was the awakening of my soul to the spiritual nourishment that is the Virgin Mary. I had always been exposed to the glorious deeds of our Heavenly Mother, but never quite fathomed her wonder in the depths of my being until this trip. There we were, in the nighttime procession of the sick, rain pouring down as though the tears of all those suffering in the world had manifested during this congregation. Light scintillated from the glimmering candles as everyone walked and sang "Ave, Ave, Ave María," praying in different languages all the while. Despite the pounding rain, everyone stood firm in their faith. People processed as though under a blanket of sun, thinking nothing of the inclement weather in the darkest of nights. The prayers resounded more powerfully than I thought humanly possible. It was in this moment that my eyes and heart were open to Our Lady. I vowed to her that I would never stop believing, keeping her close for years to come. I am so grateful to have received this kind of sustenance for the soul.

The song, "Ave, Ave, Ave María," first heard during our trip to Lourdes, permeated our lives in even the most uncommon of circumstances. For example, during my volleyball games, my mother was caught on camera singing this song, since it seemed like only divine intervention could secure us a win. Beyond the realm of middle school sports, nothing was out of reach for this song to take flight.

After Lourdes, our family made its way to Paris, France via train. Usually, taking a train is a simple transport between cities, lacking the encumbrance of airport security checkpoints and check-in counter lines. However, because we were three ladies traveling through Europe for a month, with various occasions that warranted distinctive garb, our suitcases outnumbered us. We were four individuals traveling with seven large suitcases.

Because there were so many pieces of luggage, my poor father ran out of ideas as well as patience when he was trying to finagle our suitcases in the small crevices of a French train. This time it was my father's turn to play real-life Tetris, only this time he was on level twenty-eight. Not knowing his struggle, I remember I was in the middle of reading *The Yearling*, dozing off because there was only so much excitement I could derive from the story about a young deer. I suddenly woke up to the sudden halting of the train.

Apparently, my father placed three or four of our suitcases in the "exit only" section of the gangway connection, a big "no-no" in locomotive guidelines. Suddenly, the train stopped and so did my slumber.

Unfortunately, my father was tattled on by a disgruntled short-haired Parisian lady, who signaled my father as the culprit when the enraged senior trainman inspected the scene. This was certainly more interesting than *The Yearling* so the thought of picking up my book did not even cross my mind as I watched my father resume his game of Tetris, this time with the added obstacle of maddened Frenchmen.

After a few minutes of great struggle, and the "game" somehow mastered, we resumed our journey with my father's aversion to baggage and short-haired Frenchwomen heightened.

Besides this Mediterranean cruise, my grandfather took us on other trips together as an extended family. Aside from wanting all of us to spend time with one another, he always said he wanted his grandchildren to remember him for giving them the gift of knowledge, best acquired through travel. And that, he most certainly did. The other locations to which we journeyed include Atlantis in the Bahamas one summer, New York City for another, Rome for Christmas, and London for New Year's.

The reason why we went to Rome for Christmas comes from fulfilling my beautiful mother's lifelong dream of attending the Pope's Midnight Christmas Mass in the Vatican. Having grown up watching the Mass on television on Christmas Eve, and as a woman of great faith and many dreams, my mother had always dreamt of attending the religious celebration in person. However, once my family caught wind of what was supposed to be a six-person trip to make my mother's dream a reality (a gift my grandfather wanted to extend to her due to her cancer), the rest of the family wanted to tag along. So, my mother graciously conceded to having all twenty family members join, making the prospect of attending the

Vatican's Mass that much more difficult.

But there was nothing Ana Young could not do. So, by the grace of God, and with the help of her friend working at the Guatemalan Embassy in the Holy See, my mother secured twenty passes to attend the Pope's Midnight Christmas Mass in St. Peter's Basilica in 2010. As if that were not enough, she also managed to secure two passes to receive Holy Communion from Pope Benedict XVI himself. Rather than taking one of those passes, she gave both to her parents, who appeared on Italian TV later that evening. Other family members back in Guatemala kept calling us when they caught glimpse of my grandparents on television, leaving half the country stunned by another Ana Young miracle.

Her thirst and hunger for life not only made our travels that much more memorable, but also enriched our everyday lives with nutrients far superior to superfoods. No twenty-four hours were ever mundane, and no day was ever bland.

*My beautiful Queen with her new
Titanic purse and the Queen of England
with a local in Cork, Ireland.*

CHAPTER EIGHT

# The Queen

## Chin up.

DECEMBER 8, 2003

When Ana Young is your mother, you find yourself hearing Great Britain's national anthem more than most. "God Save the Queen" becomes your personal mantra, striving to live your life in pursuit of Her Majesty's happiness and satisfaction.

To provide some context regarding the adequacy of the royal classification, I must take you back to my grandfather and when my mother was little. My grandfather, having been raised in the World War II era, grew up admiring the tenacity and resilience of the British Empire.

"'We shall fight on the beaches, we shall fight on the landing grounds, we shall fight in the fields and in the streets, we shall fight in the hills; we shall never surrender,'" my grandfather, maneuvering his "walking stick," quoted Winston Churchill as he called for the "lift."

This wartime fascination coupled with the dignity and propriety so characteristic of the English nobility led my grandfather to acquire an appreciation for the Crown far beyond other Guatemalan gentlemen of his time. As an honorable man of great intellect, Abuelo's captivation with historic figures, such as Winston Churchill and Margaret Thatcher, pervaded his household.

I can only imagine the pride he felt when my mother married my dad, whose father was of British descent (hence the last name Young). I also cannot even fathom the exhilarating joy my grandfather experienced when he crossed paths with Prince Charles (now King Charles III) on one of his trips to London. Just as my mother was never guided by fear, my grandfather did what most would be too afraid to do.

He approached the prince, and said with an air of great confidence, "May I shake hands with you, sir?"

Prince Charles smiled, and responded, "Of course!"

And so, after shaking hands with His Royal Highness, Abuelo patted the prince on the back as though they were old pals and said, "Good luck to you, Sir."

Upon witnessing a stranger extend physical contact with the Prince of Wales, one of the frenzied bodyguards came up to him and claimed, "You know you are the only person I know who has touched a member of the Royal Family and is still alive."

My seventy-one-year-old grandfather, stunned at the words of the worried constable, was relieved to one, still be alive, and two that Prince Charles reacted the way he did. Because if he had not responded so warmly, my grandfather said he would have written off England and left the country immediately.

Aside from the rich history, my family's genealogy, and the British monarchy, Abuelo was also captivated by other cultural facets, especially music. For example, every time he listened to the song "There'll Always Be an England," by Vera Lynn, my grandfather would become quite emotional due to the powerful lyrics regarding England's stalwart existence. And thus, for his eightieth birthday present, I burned a CD with his favorite British pieces and anthems, the only compilation of music he would hear for months on end, my grandmother claims. It was the least I could do for my other greatest hero.

My mother, having been exposed to such adoration and having always looked up to her father, developed the same enchantment with Great Britain. By observing and acknowledging the tremendous value of the royalty at the onset of childhood, my mother naturally felt elated to be referred to as a queen.

 The title, however, could also not have felt more perfect and natural in designating due to her natural elegance and class. I remember other mothers at The Academy used to comment on how my mother never looked disheveled. Even during a Girl Scouts trip to Savannah, Georgia, my mother and sister shared a room with a close friend and her mother, Kelsey and Susan Langston. Susan could not believe how put together my mother looked, even in the mornings and at night. Her sense of sophistication and dignified demeanor cultivated a reputation that preceded her. She was regal in all forms, a life comparable to that of Saint-Saën's *Symphony No. 3*, his grand organ symphony, fit for a Queen. The majestic sounds of string and powerful pounds of pipes overwhelm even the most ambivalent of individuals. Just as when you hear this piece, when Ana Young walks into the room, you cannot help but cease all activities and gaze in disbelief at the magnificence before you.

 I will never forget the day upon which we established her royal title, naturally given by birth, but officially decreed across the Gulf of Mexico. I always made it a point to make my beautiful mother's happiness a priority.

 "Chin up," I signaled, literally using the plane's tea stirrer to lift her chin in an upward motion.

 Because we were heading back to Tampa from spending Christmas vacation in Guatemala, my mother was faced with the sadness normally felt from departing her immediate family and childhood home. Sensing this contentment impediment, I began to attempt to cheer her up with the limited resources available to a passenger of a plane with the seatbelt sign turned on. And thus, I grabbed the stirrer and after a few minutes of creative discourse regarding her chin and its anti-gravitational pull, she was smiling and laughing as before. "Chin up" became a new mantra between the two of us, serving as a reminder to continuously keep optimism at the forefront.

 In a further attempt to add to her joy, I crafted a game of

hangman. The answer to the puzzle was "I love you, My Queen!" You could sense her jubilation as she guessed each letter, drawing nearer and nearer to the final result. Her reaction once she revealed the phrase was synonymous to me finding out there were chocolate chip cookies in the house. To the common man, her reaction seemed as though she had just won an all-expenses-paid vacation to the Bahamas for guessing the Prize Puzzle on *Wheel of Fortune*. But to my mother, having her daughter reach an appellation so fitting and flattering was far more fulfilling. And thus, from that day forward, she was and shall always be, my beautiful Queen.

---

It was the desire to make her happy that led to the cultivation of our beautiful friendship. As a little girl, I remember my mom always asking my father for foot massages due to her long days upkeeping our wonderful home. Picking up on this need, I would offer my services to My Queen for a few reasons. One, because I loved her so much, and two because her feet were just the cutest things I had ever seen. Not only were they in the most perfect condition, they were the smallest adult human feet I have ever seen. As a size five and a half, my mother's "Cinderella feet" became one of my favorite parts about her. They symbolized her undeniable cuteness, along with all the hard work she put forth for her family.

I should note that I do not have a thing for feet, by any means. Just ask my sister. Her foot so much as touches my leg and I immediately shut down and lose all focus on the outside world. But when my mom's feet would come across my path? I welcomed them with open arms. They were one more beautiful component of one of God's most perfect creations.

Another example of always trying to make her happy involves the commonplace act of sneezing.

"When I go to college, I'm going to miss saying 'bless you' every single time my mom sneezes," I immediately started crying as I articulated the strangest words of my graduating class's annual Mother-Daughter Dinner senior video.

Usually, seniors talked about how they were going to miss their mother's cooking or how grateful they were for all the sacrifices made. So, did my statement come across as peculiar? Perhaps. But for me, it meant the world. My mother always appreciated the fact that after every sneeze, I would be the only one in our immediate family to offer blessings, ranging from six to as much as twelve times. Witnessing my beautiful mother sneeze twelve times in a row whilst operating a moving vehicle caused more concern than it did blind adoration. But more often than not, it was another component of our friendship, a mutual appreciation of a common curtesy so often overlooked by others, coupled with our desires to bestow good health to the other. It was also just another incredibly cute part of her persona.

Another representation of my unequivocal allegiance to my mother was the fact that I was her assistant as a little girl. From my very first memories, I recall taking it upon myself to serve as my mother's agenda book, tasked with remembering details of certain errands we had to run or places we had to visit. When we would go shopping, usually at Talbot's, I became my mother's own personal salesclerk, taking full responsibility for finding the cream chiffon skirt in a different size, for example. Need help with the zipping? Boom, I was there. Need the dress in another color? Came back with three. Despite not being offered a job by the impressed merchants at Talbot's, I remember how happy and honored I was when My Queen called me her assistant, thanking me for my services and efficient help. I proudly held the title and carried out the position to the best of my abilities at all times and in all locations.

Beyond the realm of shopping complexes, I was her assistant at home as well. For example, my beautiful mother loved shoes. For some reason, however, she never had the time to organize her quite extensive shoe closet, leaving piles of slippers, sneakers, and pumps in a disorderly array. Thus, it was always a challenge to find the pair of her desired shoe.

Again, I do not have a thing for feet, but you better believe that when my mother needed my help in diving into the sea of forlorn footwear,

I was the first one she'd call. The sense of satisfaction when I found the matching shoe was too great to pass up. And yes, this time, there was in fact, a shoe.

Another small way I'd serve my mother was through the random acts of giving her bubble gum or peanut butter M&M's (and no, I'm not advocating for the mixture of the two. I'm no heathen). If I ever were to encounter a specific type of candied bubble gum and/or peanut butter M&M's, I would save them for her because I knew they were her favorite. I'm talking Halloween, prizes at the dentist, office candy, you name it. If I came across either item, I didn't even bother thinking about choosing my favorite, Hershey's Special Dark Chocolate bar, at the top of the pile. It was more satisfying ascertaining the Queen's happiness than indulging in any piece of chocolate.

This need to please and serve my mother extended beyond my youth. As I grew older, our incredible bond only became stronger due to our mutual understanding and admiration for one another. We appreciated the same things, sought excellence in all, and held like values in our life approach. Just as my mother received the distinction of honor roll during every opportunity at school, I too made it a point to secure all twenty honor rolls during my grade school tenure. Just as she worked hard to distinguish herself academically in high school, I too placed the utmost importance on scholastic obligations, leading me to achieve an undergraduate degree in business at the University of Notre Dame. Just as she worked tirelessly to secure tremendous results in the working world, I too have taken it upon myself to devote countless hours to the positions I've held with General Mills. She has been a pillar and guide for me since the very beginning.

When Ana Young is your mother, you begin a fascination with languages that leads you to other worlds and cultures. Her appreciation of different dialects inspired me to pursue the study of French and Italian in high school and college. I first started with French in high school, continuing its study at Notre Dame and by living in Paris for the immersion program I mentioned previously. Due to my self-imposed goal, set in the eighth grade, of learning Italian and living for a time in Italy, I pursued a minor in the language at Notre Dame and studied abroad for a semester in Rome.

Having developed fluency in both languages through a wide array of classes and experiences, I learned a myriad of songs. Songs that I could not simply keep to myself, and thus occasionally showcased my musical repertoire around the house as I performed daily activities. Unlike my sister, who would usually advocate for my silence, my beautiful mother loved this about me, acknowledging how special it was to be able to burst into song in multiple languages. Noticing her affinity for such an activity, whenever my mother needed a pick-me-up, I sang "La vie en rose" by Edith Piaf, "Le festin" from the movie *Ratatouille*, or "Volare" by Domenico Mondugno, to name a few. I usually tried to stay away from opera because I liked our glassware too much to risk its demise, but I will say I dabbled with Puccini on occasion.

A crowd favorite was always France's national anthem, "La Marseilles," because my mother would always start singing along. My roots of performing in front of family members came in handy because you better believe my mother would request that I sing in my various languages in front of my grandparents, aunts, uncles, and cousins. But if the Queen requested it, her wish was most certainly my command.

One afternoon, after a round of singing, I went into my parent's room where she was resting, looking through her piles of magazines in bed in her oversized Tampa Bay Lightning tee shirt. As I approached to give her a hug, she stops me suddenly.

"Cath," she said with a loving and concerned glance.

"Yes, My Mommy?" I asked, wondering why she looked at me so.

"*Por favor, siempre cuídese, tu vales mucho* (Translation: Please always take care of yourself. You are worth so much)" she said to me one night, pointing out my ability with languages, experiences, and accomplishments I had already attained as a young lady of twenty-three.

I remember these words struck me, because I hadn't really thought about all my achievements at once until My Queen underscored their significance.

"*No todos hacen lo que usted ya ha hecho.*" (Translation: Not everyone does what you've already done)."

I'll never forget this moment because I felt as though I had reached a point of fulfillment. Here was my hero, lauding me for my life efforts. I could not help but feel an immeasurable sense of peace.

If my self-confidence ever needs tending, I think of this conversation and immediately realize just how well-equipped I am to tackle life due to the guidance and example my beautiful mother set for me.

I could tell how proud of me she was, proud to be my mother, and proud to have a daughter that not only followed in her footsteps, but also made dreams of hers a reality. One of these dreams included writing a book.

"Cath, I want to write a book about my life. I think it would help others. Can you help me?" She asked one perfect Sunday morning.

"Yes, of course my beautiful Queen," I responded, trying to hide my excitement from her.

Little did she know I had already started writing this book. Like My Mommy, I had always dreamt of writing one. The subject did not become clear to me until 2018. I had this incredible story of resilience and love right in front of me, and knew it had to be shared with the world. Wanting to keep the project a secret so it could be revealed later as a surprise, I told her I would aid her in her efforts to compile a novel. The dream, however, was brought to fruition three years later.

As I have mentioned, my beautiful mother and I shared the same love of life and love of Christmas.

One of my favorite memories serving my sweet mother naturally involved the most magical time of the year: Christmas. On the day after Thanksgiving in 2018, I wanted to surprise my beautiful Queen with decorating the entire house for Christmas, something I knew she would most certainly appreciate. And so, as my other family members left to reap the discounts of Black Friday, I stayed home to take care of my angel. As the Queen napped, I knew I had roughly two hours to turn our house into a Winter Wonderland. And thus, with my sneakers on and my can-do attitude in place, I somehow pulled it off, nearly risking my life on several occasions due to the large unwieldy tree I had to carry up the stairs to self-assemble. I filled the house with lights and even made cookies as the *Yule Log* crackled on the television of our Florida home.

    I will never forget my beautiful mother's face illuminate as she walked out of her room and gazed at the glistening garlands, and radiant strings of light that filled our house. It felt as though we were in the scene of a Hallmark movie. Few moments have been so special in my entire life. To give my mother a surprise sprinkle of the joy and magic of Christmas was all I could ever ask for.

    Not only did I always want to serve My Queen, but I also always wanted to look like her. One day as a little girl, as my mother stood in my room at the foot of my bed, I remember thinking to myself, "Wow my mom looks like a cartoon. She's so pretty and perfect." That's because she was. Her hair was always perfectly combed, her smile radiant, her eyes scintillating, and her soul beaming with warmth to top it all off. How could she get any prettier? The answer is she couldn't. Even as I grew older, I thought my mother was more beautiful than any movie star I had ever seen on television. You may think it's an exaggeration, but there was something in her smile and in her warm gaze that perfectly encapsulated the word "beauty."

    When I was little, I had an accident. I fell after playing in the water of a fountain in my grandparents' summer home in Antigua, Guatemala. Upon falling, it didn't occur to me to place my hands in front to break my fall, as any normal human would do. Instead, I decided to let my teeth break my fall. Letting me down in more ways than one, my teeth were not victorious against Newton's Third Law of Motion, cracking down the middle and leaving me looking like a hockey player in the Stanley Cup playoffs. Unfortunately, those affected were my two front adult teeth, making a bloody gaping hole in the middle of my mouth. I immediately started to cry, running towards My Mommy.

Upon arriving, the first thing I said through my sanguinary sobbing, "Mommy, I'm not going to look like you anymore."

I was devastated. I truly thought I had lost my teeth for good, meaning I would never look like my idol with her immaculate smile.

Thankfully, I was rushed to the dentist and did not have to result to dentures. And because my mother's old friend was the dentist, he comped the entire operation and we ended up not having to pay a dime. My grandmother and mother left crying due to this kind gesture, as I dealt with flashbacks of the Barney incident.

To this day, the greatest compliment anyone could ever give me is stating that I look like my darling mother. To me, not only was she the human embodiment of physical perfection, but also, she had the perfect voice. When she spoke on the phone, in person, or sang, her voice hit sounds that can only be explained by the ethereal.

Because of the dulcet quality of her voice, I on occasion will still listen to the numerous voicemails she left me, always ending the messages with the sweetest "love yous" and "bye-byes."

You can imagine when she sang karaoke. My father, sister, and I would lose our minds when she grabbed the microphone to sing "Anduriña" by Juan y Junior or "Somewhere Over the Rainbow" from the *Wizard of Oz*. We listened in auditory amazement with her beautiful smile and eyes scintillating as the words levitated in rhythmic wonder.

As a little girl, I remember I felt as though I was quite literally attached to my mother. Everywhere we went, there I was, latched on to her arm as though my bodily functioning depended on it.

This desire to always be near her also led me to constantly traverse the living room and kitchen in the middle of the night, to make my way to the solace of my mother's embrace after daily nightmares plagued my sleep. My poor father did not quite appreciate my nighttime interruption, but I could not help but seize the opportunity of entering my haven, clinging onto my mother for the entirety of the night. Despite waking up in a pool of sweat, my mother never pushed me away or sent me back because in her motherly wisdom and extraordinary care, she knew I needed to be there with her. This was especially important during times of duress induced by episodes of "The Doll."

One time I remember we fell asleep holding hands, referring to that instance as our "Hallmark movie moment." As I grew older, my nightmares eventually subsided. But I always took great comfort in sleeping in the same bed with My Queen. There was this incredible sense of peace as we both dozed off into deep slumber. So, whenever I was stressed, sad, or just needed some sort of pick-me-up, I always asked to spend the night with my dearest friend. And without fail or hesitation, she always answered yes.

This sense of serenity also applied to times when I did not sleep in the same bed with My Queen. During my formative years, I would ask my mother if she would sit and wait with me until I dozed off. The kind of patience it takes for someone to wait for me to fall asleep can only be described by an unwilling spectator at a rainy Notre Dame football game in November. The conditions miserable, and the timing longer than desired.

Beyond the adventures of sleep, without my beautiful angel, an overwhelming sensation of fear and ambiguity plagued my childhood psyche. One day, my mother went bike riding with my grandfather in Antigua. While they rode off, my grandmother was tasked with taking care of me and my sister. She recounts that while my mother was away, I experienced a tantrum of panic.

"Where's my Mommy? Why didn't she tell me where she was going?

How could she have left me?" I questioned in between tears and strained breaths.

My grandmother very sweetly and understandingly stated, "Yes, you are right, she should have told you she was leaving, but she told me. How about we go and look for her?"

This sounded reasonable enough, even though it was Holy Week in Antigua and attempting to maneuver a vehicle with masses of people lining the pavement to see processions was a rookie mistake. But nothing was going to come between me and My Mommy.

Despite the crowded streets, Abuela and I hopped in a car to search for My Queen. As anticipated, the crowds were so dense that our car got stuck in the multitude, and my beautiful mom made it home before we did. The fear and panic then transferred to her since she didn't know where one of her daughters had gone. Abuela and I finally made our way home and upon reuniting, all was well with the world again.

This same panic transpired one time during Gasparilla, Tampa's annual pirate festival, which greatly resembles Mardi Gras due to the beads and parades. Thus, you can imagine the hordes of people flooding the streets due to the revelry.

As a family, we have taken part in the celebration every year since I was a little girl. One of my first memories during this time was the most traumatizing. Wanting to mobilize and obtain a good location to see the annual parade, we decided to switch to the other side of the street. Upon crossing, my father and I were separated from my mother and sister by a disgruntled police officer whose primary focus was to keep the drunkards at (Tampa) bay. To keep the family together, my father tried explaining to the police our need to stay together. It only took a few seconds for my sense of panic to kick in. I immediately started crying at the fear of being apart from my mother. Like a recovering alcoholic, my tears and apparent breakdown finally convinced the officer to concede, and we joined My Queen. We were complete once again.

Although I was only about eight years old, I vividly remember this moment in time as if it occurred just yesterday. It also captures just how much I needed to be with my dear mother. This fear of losing her was a constant theme in my childhood. I remember watching the movie *Titanic* for the first time, bawling my eyes out because I pictured losing my mother at sea. At that time in my life, I could have cared less if Jack and Rose ended up together. My sole focus was if I were on a sinking ship, I could not get separated from my best friend. Her role in my life extended beyond that of motherhood. I needed My Mommy like I needed to breathe.

When Ana Young is your mother, your go-to phrase becomes "I love you, My Mommy."

One day, we were in the kitchen of my childhood home, and I was still not tall enough to reach the counter for cookies, I remember saying in a burst of joy, "I love you, My Mommy" as she reached for the little brown treasures.

My beautiful mother, overtaken by the sounds of these words coupled with my youthful cuteness, shared, *"Awww! Me derrito cada vez que me dices 'My Mommy'"* (Translation: I melt every time you call me 'My Mommy!') she shared, hugging me with the palpable love of her motherly affection.

I took a mental note of the power of these words and vowed to utilize them whenever possible. So much so, that when I fell asleep every night, I wanted the last thing I would say to be these words in case something happened to me overnight. Moreover, God forbid something would happen to My Queen, I wanted the last words she would hear from me to be her favorite phrase. (In retrospect, it probably was not a good idea to watch *The Titanic* after all.) Regardless, it became tradition. For numerous years, the last thing I would say before going to sleep was "I love you, My Mommy" for all the reasons explained above. I realize how dramatic I sounded as a young girl of six, but my love for My Queen, coupled with an aversion to risk transcended all logic.

I have always perceived life differently than most. I have always been keenly aware of the finiteness of our life on Earth. I remember as a little girl in the first grade telling myself to enjoy watching television because I somehow knew this freedom of time and energy was transient.

"Catherine when you get older, you're not going to be able to watch TV as much, so enjoy it now while you can," I said to myself.

I was seven.

Granted, as a working woman in my late-twenties, I have found more time to take part in this entertainment activity yet again, usually watching episodes of *The Office* every evening before going to sleep. However, it was this unique truth of childhood freedom that I held at the forefront of my thoughts, leading me to appreciate the present more so than most little girls.

Another profound life truth I kept in the back of my mind was the fact that I knew I wouldn't have my parents around forever, and thus had to cherish the time with them as much as possible. I used to stop randomly in the middle of studying or doing homework to run over and hug my sweet mother due to these thoughts of fleeting time. It's also why I constantly would thank her for my wonderful life. I know it sounds morose to have had these inklings since I was a child, but in actuality it provided me with an unending sense of gratitude for the present, allowing me to bask in the beauty of My Queen and soak her in as much as possible.

It's like I knew deep down how precious time with her was, and so I made it a priority to enjoy her presence as much as humanly possible.

And that I did. I have no regrets. I have peace in knowing I loved her to the extreme, cherished her more than most, and adored her in the best way I could.

If writing this book wasn't any indication, I cherished the relationship between me and my mother more than anything in this world. It extended beyond a traditional mother-daughter friendship. It was a mutual appreciation for each other, a gratitude for the wonderful life and opportunities she provided, especially the irrefutably impeccable example she set.

When I was two years old, my beautiful Queen was diagnosed with breast cancer. Rather than sharing this knowledge with me and my elder sister, my mom, to shield us from the pain and worry, kept it a secret for fifteen years. She would drive us to school, go to various chemotherapy, radiation, and doctor appointments, and then pick us up as if nothing was wrong. She did this for years without ever complaining or putting herself first.

When her breast cancer came back my freshman year at Notre Dame, having metastasized to her lungs, my father sat me down and told me everything: all the suffering she went through, the courage she possessed, and the optimism that ultimately saved her life.

When I was a little girl, there were times when I felt it was necessary to cry. For example, in the spirit of childhood naivety, if I wanted to prove a point with my parents or gain sympathy through a demonstration of emotion, I would try and make myself cry. I knew only one thing could instantly do the trick: thinking about losing my mother. Instant tear-jerker. So, you can imagine the flow of tears when I thought it could actually happen. One of the hardest moments in my life.

After that conversation with my father, I entered my dimly lit home with a twinge of uneasiness as I approached my parent's room. As I entered and witnessed the most perfect human being sitting in the middle of the bed with her oversized Mickey Mouse tee-shirt, pearls, perfect hair, and the largest smile on her beautiful face, the tears started flowing even heavier now. She looked wonderful, and I gained some sense of relief that everything would be fine.

Thankfully, her cancer at that time was slow-growing, and her treatments were not as extreme as the ones she had experienced at the onset of the disease due to the incredible research and scientific breakthroughs of our generation. Thus, for most of my college experience, we would forget my mother had such a horrific disease due to her aura of sunshine that shone through like the most luminescent of lights in the darkest of nights, a contrast unfathomable to most.

On our final trip to Notre Dame my senior year, when my mother stayed after my graduation to help me move out of my apartment, a song from the Italian film, *Life is Beautiful*, started playing in the car. It was in that moment that I started crying because I realized the parallels of the movie with my fearless mother in my own life.

For those of you who have not seen the film, please take the time to do so. To avoid spoiling the plot, I will keep the explanation high-level. Just as the father in the film protected his son from the harsh realities of the concentration camp, my mother safeguarded our childhood innocence by battling her ferocious cancer without our knowledge.

Every little girl thinks their mom is Superwoman, but I didn't know mine actually was. I thank my mom every day for not telling me about her cancer for sixteen years, because it would have absolutely destroyed the light that permeated my childhood. Instead, thanks to my mother's wisdom, foresight, and courageous heart, my childhood was one you hear about in storybooks. It was a beautiful compilation of times filled with love and laughter, times of chocolate chip cookies and trips to Disney World, times without worry or pain. If two-year-old me knew there was a chance of losing my beautiful best friend, I don't know where I would be today.

Life is like a secret garden, each of us finding the hidden patch of life behind every closed gate. Just as the winter months melt their wintry frost into a beautiful springtime, no matter how daunting an obstacle or chapter may appear, one inevitably blooms again.

A classic Ana-Catherine moment that captures this philosophy occurred when we watched the movie *Mary Poppins Returns* in Cinebistro. It is our favorite movie theater where you eat gourmet foods and drink to your heart's content while watching movies. I was so overtaken by the beautiful sights and sounds of the film, even crying at the end due to the profound messaging of the song, "There's Nowhere to Go but Up." Both of us left the theater with happy hearts and large smiles. After exclaiming our admiration and fondness of the film upon exiting, my sister and father gave the movie two thumbs down, claiming it was not very well done. As I stood aghast at such commentary, I knew my mother understood my vantage point better than anyone else. At the end of the day, despite the harsh realities of a sometimes-unforgiving world, there's joy and hope in even the most dire situations. I couldn't help but draw parallels to our present reality. Despite the incredibly heart wrenching period we were facing as a family, there was always light at the end of the tunnel, with *nowhere to go but up.*

During the subsequent months, unsurprisingly, I failed to find a singular person who shared this same view towards the film. To this day, I still hold onto the string of my "balloon," "waltzing on air" with my beautiful mother, laughing and singing along to the lifelong melody of this extraordinary perspective: chin up, for there's no other direction to go.

*My mother and I
in front of the Morris Inn,
with what would become her tree at the
University of Notre Dame.*

**CHAPTER NINE**

# Gold Leaf

*What I know is that God is always there.*

**MAY 28, 2018**

When Ana Young is your mother, you learn the perpetuity of laughter. You become a witness to the human incarnate of sunshine, without the onus of UV ray exposure. You become an observer to the healing powers of her smile, the soft soothing melody of her voice, and the unbelievable comfort in experiencing such beauty. Her smile had a healing power to cure all notions of negativity, and her melodic voice soothed the uneasiness of daily toil. Some would say she was a walking Disney character. She was like an inextinguishable light that bounced and flickered to incessantly radiate joy to all who knew her.

It is her inner joy that led her to love Disney, which in turn drove her desire to expose such magic to her daughters. Despite my father's complaints about "going to visit the mouse again," without those trips to the Happiest Place on Earth, I am convinced I would be a completely different person.

Perhaps I wouldn't be so drawn to sugar and parades had I not frequented Disney at a young age. But it goes beyond the pomp and circumstance of a theme park experience. Disney focuses on the good and inculcates positive life lessons to children at a very young age. These include pursue your dreams, go the distance, love and honor your parents, and trust in the incontestable fact that good always triumphs over evil.

Some pessimists like to point out that these lessons are only setting up children for a lifetime of disappointment and frustration. Some realists state that said lessons should only belong in the world of childish naivety. However, my mother believed that these pessimistic statements are simply mere claims to a deeper and more profound ignorance of real life. Why not go the distance? Why not focus on the good? Yes, life is hard, but without the right mindset, it becomes infinitely harder.

    As in the 1979 film, *Life of Brian*, one should "always look on the bright side of life." My mother lived this out each day. Even after every chemotherapy infusion and after each radiation treatment she would thank God for the beautiful life she had, acknowledging the bountiful blessings He had bestowed upon her.

    When Ana Young is your mother, you're willing to spend five thousand dollars on a tree. I know what you're thinking, is this tree made from *gold leaf*? In reality, this tree is built upon an even more precious substance: faith.

    Faith is one of the cornerstones of Ana. Her most admirable quality, one could argue. Because it was so strong, you'd think her faith was a side effect of some tangible occurrence, like the time when she quickly downed three bottles of holy water at TSA due to the forbidden nature of liquid on planes and her refusal to waste the precious substance. But no, it was not a specific instance in time, rather there were several events throughout her life that caused her faith to strengthen and grow.

    One of these times includes when my mother was in her early thirties. The doctors in Guatemala found a few tumors around her uterus in 1990, and thus suggested its removal. My unmarried mother knew, however, that she wanted to have kids of her own one day, and thus sought a second opinion, praying fervently all the while to complete her destiny of becoming a mom. Thankfully, once at Johns Hopkins, my mother's doctors recommended the removal of just the tumors, leaving the uterus intact as well as her ability to birth both me and my sister, a miracle she lovingly mentioned throughout our lives. This trip is also what sparked the romance of my parents since my father was also living in Maryland at the time. Another great reminder that everything does indeed happen for a greater purpose.

My mother's steadfast faith in God was anything but a secret. Specifically, my beautiful Queen would speak of the healing powers of the Virgin of Fátima in Portugal.

For those unfamiliar with the story, the Virgin Mary, Mother of God, appeared to three little children in Fátima, a quaint little town in the western part of Portugal. At the time of her apparitions, there was great uncertainty and civil unrest in the world. To share the Good News, restore faith, and ultimately preserve peace, the Virgin of Fátima proceeded to appear to the children on the thirteenth of every month for six consecutive months in 1917. Today, Fátima is considered a holy place, once graced with the Blessed Mother's visits.

The parallelism of the story to my beautiful mother's life strengthened the bond with her celestial mother. As aforementioned, the thirteenth of the month was when the Virgin would appear. Having been born on the thirteenth of February, my mother celebrated the thirteenth of every month as a day of great joy and blessings. Despite popular culture's negative portrayal of thirteen as an omen of misfortune, my mother brushed this off as ignorant, secular attempts to tarnish religious integrity. And thus, her love of the number flourished alongside her belief in God.

The relationship between the Virgin of Fátima extends beyond numeric symbolism. The fascination with all things Mary dates back to her childhood. Having been raised in a Catholic family, my mother had the example of her parents to guide her along her faith journey. Both of her parents were steadfast believers and admirers of the Virgin Mary. My grandmother was even named after Her, Concepción, after the Immaculate Conception. Having had this example of zealous Mary admiration, my mother's first true encounter with the power of Mary's influence occurred when my mother was thirty-three. After having gone through intense emotional turmoil due to a break-up with someone whom my mother thought was "the one," my mother asked Mary for a sign that all would be well with the world again. Later that evening, my mother had a dream in which the Virgin of Guadalupe appeared to her in a dream, stating, *"Espere grandes acontecimientos."* (Translation: Expect great events). A month later, my father appeared, and they were married shortly after. With the Virgin's promise fulfilled, my mother's faith only grew from then on.

When my mother was first diagnosed with cancer at the age of forty, she turned to the Virgin of Fátima because at the very moment my mother asked God for a sign that all was going to be ok, someone gave her a beautiful image of the Virgin. That was her sign, and from then on, my mother pledged her devotion to Fátima, never ceasing to believe in her power and receiving so many miracles because of her devotion. Her persistence with sharing all the miracles Our Lady granted her inspired countless individuals.

First and foremost, she inspired her family. We were the firsthand witnesses to her incredible faith and the miracles that occurred daily. Every little victory that most would consider happenstance was attributed to an act of God. For example, my mother always found a parking spot no matter how busy or bustling the location. Rather than attributing the phenomenon to luck, it was the Virgin Mary who found my mother a parking spot near the front of Macy's at noon on Black Friday.

My father, on the other hand, did not experience the same type of blessing when tasked to park. If he was driving, we all knew to wear comfortable walking shoes.

Although married to one of God's most faith-filled servants, my father's faith was not as strong as hers. Perhaps it was the realist in him that caused the struggle in believing completely. Regardless, he was always captivated by the beauty of my mother's unwavering belief in God, making him a better man because of it.

Faith of course extended beyond the parking lot. Whenever

something would go missing, my mother, without hesitation or apprehension, comforted the family members whose object had gone missing by sweetly stating, *"No se preocupen. Va a aparecer. Yo le voy a rezar a la Virgen de Fátima. Ella nos va a hacer el milagro."* (Translation: Don't worry. It will turn up. I'm going to pray to the Virgin of Fátima. She will grant us a miracle)." And sure enough, after about twenty minutes, the object would appear, and peace once again would be restored.

Her unwavering belief in the Virgin of Fátima led even the most skeptical of humans to perceive religion differently. First, my beautiful mother never traveled anywhere without her image of the Virgin set in a miraculous frame. Yes, you read that correctly, even the frame has a corresponding miracle. Upon obtaining the picture, my mother searched high and low for the perfect enclosure of our Heavenly Mother. One day, a family friend gave her a frame that fit the image perfectly as if specially manufactured for this very photograph. Another miracle to make its way into daily conversations with strangers.

My mother made it a point to spread her faith, regardless of location or circumstance. From check-outs at department stores to random run-ins at gas stations, my mother knew the power of faith and the wealth one would gain from her wisdom. Therefore, she never stopped sharing it with the world.

The great Winston Churchill once said, "Never was so much owed by so many to so few." My mother was the few. He of course was referring to the British fighter pilots that valiantly defended Great Britain during a time of great peril. But I like to think Churchill also knew the impact my mother's faith would have on so many.

When my mother was first diagnosed with cancer, she prayed incessantly to the Virgin Mary, asking the Blessed Mother to extend her life so that my earthly mother could set an example for others and spread the Good News of God. And she did exactly this. With my beautiful mother's life extended twenty-three wonderful years, wherever she found herself, whether at Dillard's or at our local Shell, she shared how enriching believing in God and the Virgin Mary is on a person's existence.

She also promised the Virgin Mary that she would take her daughters to Fátima if she were to survive, to promote our faith and pay homage to the miracle.

For years I heard about Fátima, about how my mother wanted to take me and my sister to one of the most awe-inspiring places in the world. And for years I envisioned my mother's relationship with the Virgin of Fátima simplistic, contextualized in parking spots, grateful relatives, and the number thirteen. I had no idea there was a far greater purpose for traveling to Portugal.

Once I uncovered the truth about my mother's health, so many things started to make sense. The faint memory of a wig my dad used to put on playfully around the house to make us smile, the overnight mystery surgery that almost killed me from separation anxiety, the abrupt end to being carried in my beautiful mother's arms at a young age, and of course the *miracles* my mother spoke of day in and day out. The unbelievable sacrifices she made to protect our childhood and emotional wellbeing could not have been carried out without her faith.

Miracles, both large and small, filled her life and guided her to unlock the unattainable. So, whether it was the incontrovertible fact that my mother always found amazing parking, to beating cancer twice, so many things transpired in my mother's life to solidify her wholehearted faith in God and the Virgin Mother.

My mother truly believed miracles happened every day. It's the reason why she loved and chose the song, "Miracles Happen" from the movie *The Princess Diaries* for me and my sister to perform at our all-school talent show.

It was her faith that preserved her beautiful life for twenty-three spectacular years. Her belief in a greater power, a reason for being, and the ultimate comfort in knowing our life on earth is as transient as the sand in the sea, directly correlates with the inspiring way she lived.

What does this all have to do with a tree? I'll explain. When my mother was a little girl, she dreamt with God. In the dream, God was an enormous, beautifully majestic tree, with life and light emanating from its impressive branches. Now, what exactly occurred in the dream remains a mystery. But my mother was so struck by the nighttime apparition, that for the entirety of her life, she associated God with trees. Which, if you think about it, makes sense. The fact that trees are part of His creation, coupled with their oxygen-producing qualities, and God breathes life into every one of us, further prompted my mother to hold this religious-arbor correlation. To promote the *blooming* of my mother's health and support her beautiful faith during her onerous battle in an environment full of God, I donated money to the University of Notre Dame to have a tree dedicated to my Queen.

This is just another example of the premise *everything happens for a reason*. If I had not worked in the Notre Dame Development Office all four years of college, I would not have known such giving opportunities existed. Even more, if I had not been co-chair of Senior Legacy, a branch of development that focuses on inspiring the senior class to leave lasting legacies in honor of their time at ND, I would not have befriended Ellen Roof, my dear friend who helped spearhead the committee and ensured the dedication of my mother's tree not only took place, but also made sure the process was expedited and executed to perfection. This involved walking around campus taking numerous pictures of potential candidates. I am forever grateful to her and to Notre Dame for my most precious gift. Located in her favorite part of the University's awe-inspiring grounds, in front of the Morris Inn on Notre Dame Avenue, the tree will remain there forever, signifying her unwavering faith and love of God. She is and will be forever immortalized.

The original plan was to unveil the commemorative gift during our next trip to ND's campus, which was supposedly on the weekend of Notre Dame's annual half marathon, *The Holy Half*, a race my mother had seen me run as a senior in college. I was incredibly excited to share this experience again with her, because this time, I wouldn't have a torn hamstring, resulting from doing the splits at my favorite bar, The Blarney Stone (or Finnis as we called it) the week prior to the last time I ran the race. However, despite my healed leg, due to my mother's treatments, her immune system was compromised, and her doctor advocated against traveling to avoid exposure to other illnesses. And so, we capitalized on the advancements of technology to present her surprise. Held moments after finishing the race, the subsequent FaceTime conversation we had will leave a permanent imprint on my soul. Standing in front of the Morris Inn, my mother's favorite place on campus due to its beauty, staff, and all the fond moments we shared there when she visited me at school, I presented the tree with all the love I could possibly share through a video call. I will never forget the tears she shed, the gratitude she experienced, and the love she felt.

All I ever wanted in life was to give her the world. And so, I thought a tree, with the following plaque inscription would do:

*To my beautiful Mother*
*Ana M. Young*
*It is through your passion for life and*
*love of God that you have changed*
*countless lives for good.*
*May God and Our Lady*
*continue to bless you forever and always.*
*Catherine A. Young*

To this day, I visit her tree a few times a year. And every time I gaze at its welcoming trunk, strong branches, and charming foliage, I feel her near me, with God himself and the Virgin Mary standing by my side.

The most unbelievable thing about the tree is that when I was sifting through photos of my beautiful mother, I found a picture of us standing in front of the same tree my sophomore year at Notre Dame. Because my mother loved photos, she insisted on having our photo taken in front of the tree since it radiated with colorful luminescence. Of all the trees we could have chosen to pose in front of and of all the trees I could have chosen to dedicate to my guardian angel, I happened to choose the one photographed. It is another testament to God's unending guidance.

On my last visit to Notre Dame before my mother departed this world, I stopped inside the Morris Inn to purchase a crucifix for her. One of My Queen's favorite parts about spending the night at the hotel was the beautiful crucifix near the entrance of every room. She loved the detail, coloring, and elegance of the cross, arguably Christianity's greatest symbol. To continue with my perpetual quest of service to My Queen, I wanted to surprise her with a crucifix of her very own.

Serendipitously, one of the staff members my mother knew very well, was working that afternoon at the front desk.

Two years prior, my mother wanted to stay at the highly coveted hotel during my graduation from Notre Dame, a task more improbable than dining in Cinderella's Castle. However, in classic Ana Young fashion, no possibility was ever an improbability, so she proceeded to call the Morris Inn every day for a year. That's right, Liam, as well as other hotel staff, spoke to my mother over 365 times. As the weekend drew near, one of the managers mentioned the rooms were blocked for large donors and other elite personnel that came to visit campus, e.g., Vice President Mike Pence who gave my class's commencement address. The manager told her to speak with the Development Office since they usually had rooms reserved for other reasons as well. My mother, because of her insistence and determination in calling every day was able to receive this information and relayed the message to me.

I'll never forget the phone call. I was studying in LaFortune Student Center, or LaFun, in my usual booth in front of Subway, when I responded to the news, "Mom… I work in the Development Office."

And so, I texted my dear friend Ellen, asked if we could have a few rooms for my family, and she immediately said yes, inquiring how many we needed.

"Mom, how many do we need?" I asked, thinking only a couple would suffice.

"We need six," she responded, without any hesitation or notion of the excessiveness.

Shocked and slightly embarrassed to ask for such a tall order, I texted Ellen back with the agreed upon number.

To my great surprise and joy, she replied, "Done."

Ana Young had done it again.

Fast forward to my mission of purchasing the crucifix. Liam, who was now a manager at the Morris Inn, did not recognize me as I approached him. Once I mentioned I was the daughter of Ana Young, his face illuminated with the familiarity of my beautiful Queen.

"Yes, of course! How is she doing? We miss her here!" he exclaimed, with a newfound joy in remembering my parental connection.

Fighting to respond to his question, I immediately broke down into tears. He quickly came around the counter, and I explained the situation and my purpose for visiting. His face grew somber, but he ran to the back to provide me with a crucifix, free of charge.

"I will pray for her and your family. Please give her my love," Liam responded.

Collecting myself, and thanking him for his generous gift, I bid Liam farewell, wanting nothing more than to continue praying for my mother's health in front of her tree. So, with the crucifix in hand and her tree in front, I prayed, and I prayed, and I prayed some more. I also hugged the tree on several occasions, which probably confused bystanders. But I didn't care. I felt close to God there and needed to pray.

God did grant us many miracles throughout this time. The miracle of receiving a Morris Inn crucifix, the miracle of family and their presence during the journey, the miracle my father's insurance covered most hospital bills, the miracle of my mother's perspective and steadfast faith, the miracle of every extra day, hour, and minute we had to relish in the beauty of Ana Young. This is what every prayer to God did. Every conversation with God, every petition and song led to miracles both seen and unseen, the hidden miracles we don't even know about but that inevitably transpired.

Now if you don't have faith, or refuse to believe in a greater celestial power, then I urge you to remember my mother's story, and how it not only fueled her with the optimism to withstand great trials, but also enriched her journey far beyond normal human comprehension.

Because in the end, it's all about perspective. How one views the world determines ultimately how the world will view you. This is the thinking that helped shape her outlook on her cancer prognosis. This is the mentality that has allowed me to keep smiling after losing someone with so much light. I am not angry for her early departure from this world, only grateful that God let one of his most loyal angels leave His side to grace our world for sixty-three beautiful years.

If life were always straightforward, then how could we possibly grow as human beings, dynamic souls blessed by God with a life that allows us to roam the Earth and find purpose, meaning, substance?

Thank God I am a mere mortal who does not possess the encumbrance of godlike knowledge. Thank God I can just accept the fact that I will never understand why things happen the way they do, why My Queen left when she did. Thank God I can have faith and keep on living, trusting, smiling, and laughing, just as my beautiful mother did every day of her magnificent life.

You are never alone. Even as loneliness pervades your tired heart, and uneasy thoughts plague your weary mind, try and keep at the forefront of your thoughts this truth. You are never *ever* alone. God is *always* there, fighting for you to find the inner joy and light to guide your life. You are never alone. You could never be. The love of God is too strong, with times of heartache as fleeting as the darkness of night.

What is the purpose of life? Why are so many people plagued with an overpowering notion of "I can't," while others receive the bountiful blessings of apparent happenstance? The answers to such questions are not within this or any book. When the itching for us to determine why life occurs the way it does surfaces, it is when we try to become more than the mere mortals that we are. We are not God, only made in His image, finding our way through the gift of being able to feel and see and dream.

As I sit here, writing in my grandparents' beautiful Antigua home, gazing upon the magnificent mountains and impressive volcanoes, I am struck by the wonder of it all. How the highs have been so high, and the lows, so eye-opening. Eye-opening to the great today my mother so fondly sang of. For without the lows, we wouldn't have highs, and laughter, well laughter would cease altogether.

My mother always taught me to be strong. Whenever she saw me crying, she would turn, let me have my cry, but ultimately instruct me with two poignant words, "Be tough."

And so, I knew I had to be tough in the chapters that lay ahead.

125

*After she started her treatments, my beautiful mother and I at Easter brunch in Tampa.*

CHAPTER TEN

# Letters of Life

*Be tough.*

**FEBRUARY 26, 2005**

When Ana Young is your mother, you grasp the power of "Today" more profoundly than the average twenty-one-year-old. And by this, I mean two things. For one, I'm referring to the ever-present knowledge regarding the here and now, the understanding of a current reality, and the appreciation for the miracle of each day. On the other hand, I am referring to the song, "Today," written by Randy Sparks in 1964.

One day in 2016, after my usual morning run, I came home to find my sweet mother singing a song I had never heard before. Not only was I mesmerized by the sight of my beautiful mother as she sweetly sang to her two daughters in her pjs with a toothbrush in hand, but I was also struck by the song's lyrics. As she sang, she radiated each word as though imprinting them into my heart forever.

"Today, while the blossoms still cling to the vine, I'll taste your strawberries, I'll drink your sweet wine. A million tomorrows shall all pass away, ere I forget all the joy that is mine today… I can't be contented with yesterday's glories, I can't live on promises winter to spring," my beautiful mother sang, ultimately interrupted by the tears in my eyes, leading to the onset of hers.

In that moment, I could not help but cry due to an overwhelming emotion. An all-consuming adoration overpowered my heart for the beauty of my mother's soul.

It was another moment during which I felt a gratitude so pure and so tangible in the presence of My Queen, that I could not help but weep at the fact that this beautiful creature in front of me birthed me, raised me, and guided me to where I am today.

As the song suggests, it is best to focus on the present, rather than dwelling on the past and depending on the future for happiness. My mother was a living testament to this very truth. She lived a full and incredible life, loving every second of every day, basking in the miracle of being alive. Because where there is gratitude in the everyday, there is joy everlasting.

And so, the culmination of all my mother's efforts, trials, and inspiring way to live manifested itself in the final chapter of her life.

February 2018 was the time in which my greatest fear came to be… every "I love you My Mommy" nighttime fright, every goodbye I articulated to My Queen as I departed for Notre Dame, every moment of clarity in realizing the finiteness of my mother's existence as a little girl had finally reached its point of culmination. I trembled at the thought of a life without My Queen.

To fully understand the series of events that transpired, I must note that February 2018 came without forewarning, just as a bad dream unwelcomingly inserts itself into the bleak of night. I remember very vividly the day when we received news of her metastasis to the brain. I began to sob in a way only fitting for the thought of losing My Queen.

At the sight of my outcry, she turned to me and in a motherly frequency stated, "It's ok, *mi muchachita*."

And then as to explain my behavior she turns to her primary oncologist, Dr. Loftus, "It's just that she loves me very much."

It was in that moment that I felt a strange twinge of completion. I knew my mother loved me beyond measure, but it was then that I realized she knew just how much I loved her. To hear her acknowledge such love… now that is far beyond verbal explication. Every display of affection, every hug and kiss, every word of admiration and praise, reached its apex.

However oddly fulfilling it was to feel her understanding of my deep-rooted love for her, it was, as you can imagine, the single worst day of my life.

To cope with the all-consuming sadness that manifested itself in receiving such news, I did as I always do... I ran. After the hospital, I ran with so much feeling I felt that if it had not been for my heavy heart, I would have discovered human flight. I ran with an anger and fear so intense that I simply began to cry. The tears pressed hot against my cheek in the cool February afternoon. I was angry, confused, and most of all, I was petrified for what was to come.

But just when I thought my running had failed me as my coping mechanism, the endorphins crept in as fast as the tears flew off my face with each stride. Thoughts of hope flooded every crevice of my body. I began to think about the indisputable facts: I have not lost her and there is no guarantee that I will. These optimistic thoughts led me to visualize what I could control: I could enrich the difficult experience of cancer through acts of love and selflessness.

With the crescendo of pounding feet as they met the pavement and Tchaikovsky's Piano Concerto No. 1 reverberating in my ears, the fire was lit. This fire within me, this unquenchable desire to give everything I could to My Queen had settled in, stronger than ever before.

I began to ideate on what projects to embark on, what quests to take, all for the nurturing of my beautiful mother's happiness. Ultimately, I wanted to fulfill all dreams given the uncertainty of her prognosis.

Later that night, I drew up the list and started work immediately. These tasks included (not ranked in priority order):

1. Promote happiness through daily activities & outings
2. Meeting the President of the United States
3. Immortalizing her in some way
4. Birthday celebration fit for a Queen
5. Album of photos to highlight the good

      6. Letters of Life

      7. Meeting the Queen of England

      8. Spending the night in Cinderella's Castle in Disney World

Of the eight tasks, five and a half were completed. Meeting the Queen of England and spending the night in Cinderella's Castle proved to be too daunting of a task for someone who is not Ana Young. However, success emerged among the first six, which I will now explain each in greater detail:

**Task #1:** Promote happiness through daily activities & outings

Flowers… all kinds of flowers: pink roses, peach daisies, ribbons of pearl and string… every day I frequented my friendly neighborhood Publix and purchased a bouquet for My Queen. The joy and light emanating from my beautiful mother's eyes was worth more than the $11.99 spent on my daily blossoming bundle.

To ensure my mother's psyche remained elevated at all times, my family and I took it upon ourselves to maintain the happy lifestyle my mother was accustomed to before her diagnosis, bolstering it through elevated showcases of love and affection. This included Cinebistro outings, walks around Hyde Park with eighteen-year-old Millie in her stroller, trips to Disney, family members visiting from far distances, dinners at Carrabba's and PF Chang's, the aforementioned flowers I bought daily after work, and evenings watching *Wheel of Fortune* and *Jeopardy* while drinking Manhattans on the rocks, to name a few. Despite treatments and resulting side effects, my mother even found the time and energy to orchestrate my grandmother's eighty-fifth birthday gala at the Don Cesar in St. Petersburg, Florida. And not only that, she even completed a full renovation of our beach condo purchased only a few months prior.

Just as Antigua, Guatemala was her favorite place in the world, her close second (if not tied for first), was St. Pete Beach, Florida. Her love of the great expanse of water and sand coupled with our happy family memories there made my mother yearn for a piece of property to call our own. Her dream was made a reality in 2017 when we found the perfect location, an apartment complex sitting between the two hotels we used to stay in. However, because the unit itself was outdated, and my mother only wanted the best, she poured her heart and soul into renovating the space, transforming the quarters into a tropical oasis where modern meets elegant in the most seamless way. She did all this, meeting with the contractor numerous times, making several trips to home improvement stores, purchasing bedding, furniture, and small details to convert the condo into a home, all while battling the ferocious side effects of her treatments. The beach condo still stands, with all its beauty, radiating the love and foresight of my incredible mother in every crevice and corner.

Beyond the beach, her favorite leisurely activity was to go to Cinebistro. I remember this one moment in time after returning from having seen the film *First Man*. I played for my mother one of the songs of the movie's soundtrack, "Docking Waltz." A beautiful waltz composition by Justin Hurwitz that prompted my mother to stand up and dance with me, our feet seeming to levitate off the ground, as Armstrong himself did on the moon. I like to think my mother and I will one day waltz again in Heaven, soaring in rhythmic elegance to the sounds of Strauss' finest.

The quality of life extended beyond normal social gatherings and activities. Our visits to the hospital also transcended the ordinary due to my mother's beautiful way with people. Everyone loved her. All her nurses, technicians, doctors, and desk clerks knew her by name. On her birthday, she received more gifts from hospital staff than I do in two years combined. She was beloved by all.

Even during her chemotherapy appointments, my beautiful mother never stopped smiling. Due to the kindness and decency of General Mills, I was able to work remotely from the hospital every time my mother had her treatments, which culminated in incredible memories with my best friend during her infusions. We would hold philosophical discussions and candid conversations that further strengthened our bond, providing me with sound motherly advice and affection I desperately needed during such a trying time.

The most poignant moment of all her hospital visits transpired during one of my mother's overnight stays. Because of the various chemotherapies and radiation treatments my mother's body was exposed to, her mental aptitude diminished after some time, finding it hard to express rational thoughts. Always wanting to make My Queen happy, I decided to start singing to her in my different languages, just as I had done so many times before. Her beautiful smile emerged like a glowing sunrise after a tempestuous night. Her eyes wide with delight, she even started singing along with me. Pretty soon, the rest of my family joined in on the musical endeavor and we all were singing "Volare," swaying from side to side all the while. As the song title suggests (*volare* in Italian means to fly), our spirits were all flying from the joy at seeing my mother's cognitive ability rebound, coupled with such an altruistic smile. It was like a scene at the end of a Disney film, comparable to *Mary Poppins's* finale of "Let's Go Fly a Kite." The power of music manifested itself once again.

And so, the first task remained top of mind as we brought the rest of her dreams to fruition.

**Task #2:** Meeting the President of the United States

The half task I mentioned refers to dream #2. While my beautiful mother did not completely fulfill a lifelong dream of hers, that is meeting the current POTUS, she did receive a handwritten letter from President Trump as a reply to my White House correspondence. In the letter, he lauded her resilience and thanked her for setting such a model example of strength. Regardless of political leanings and legislative agenda, to receive such words from our nation's highest leader speaks volumes to the high standard with which she lived her life.

**Task #3:** Immortalization

After my grandfather's passing, my mother came up with the idea of immortalizing his legacy through having his image preserved in a commemorative bust, displayed at the company he pioneered. Knowing my mother's urge to go the extra mile and her proclivity to strive for excellence, I knew she would treasure an artifact to honor her magnificence.

And so, the dream of the tree was brought to life.

Today, she is not only immortalized at Notre Dame, but also my mother's name resides on one of the gold leaves of the *Tree of Life Honor & Memorial Society* in Holy Cross-Immaculata Church in Cincinnati, Ohio, where I currently reside. This Church is perfect for so many reasons. First, one of my mother's names is "Concepción," who like my grandmother, was named after the Immaculate Conception. Having been born on the Feast Day of the Immaculate Conception, I always felt a special bond with this designation of the Holy Mother, and the Church's name is no exception.

Second, the fact that there is a wooden tree for the memorialization of individuals, just like her beautiful tree at Notre Dame. Not only that, but the *Tree of Life* stands next to a statue of the Virgin of Fátima. On the other side, a statue of the Virgin of Lourdes with a small grotto graces this impressive space, just like the grotto at Notre Dame and Lourdes. Furthermore, this church resides in the "Queen City," a designation I associate with My Queen, my earthly mother, and the Queen of the Universe, the Virgin Mary.

I may lose some people here but I even attribute Cincinnati's area code to the Feast Day of the Virgin of Fátima, 5/13 (May thirteenth).

I know it might sound frivolous to consider such facts as signs from God. But why not believe in something greater? Why not feel the peace in discovering these truths so vivid in my heart?

For all these reasons and signs, when I moved to Cincinnati for work, and discovered this beautiful, historic Church that venerates the Virgin Mary, atop an impressive hill, I knew it was fate. Fate for me to live in the city, and fate for me to find the Church. And so, for My Queen's Christmas present in 2020, I gave her the gift of a golden leaf in this sanctified house of God.

In addition to both trees, my mom is immortalized in a third way. Thomas, our neighbor in Antigua, had a portrait made with my beautiful mother as one of the angels surrounding a magnificent antique crucifix on one of the walls of his impressive home. Underneath the crucifix lies a quote my father crafted, "Ana M. Young – Your love will light our way." Surrounded by multi-colored flowers and roses in the upper left corner, my beautiful mother's angelic body is being guided by another angel in the portrait, symbolically welcoming her to Heaven. On the bottom left, her favorite priest, Padre José Contrán, who recently passed, is the only other person featured in the artwork. It is a beautiful testament to my incredible mother, and our whole family is forever grateful.

**Task 4:** The Queen's Royal 63rd Birthday

To infuse my mother with the love and attention she deserved on her favorite day of the year, I knew we had to make her birthday extra special. As the detail-oriented lady that she was, I knew she would appreciate every element of the birthday extravaganza we had in store for her.

I remember sleeping two hours the night before due to the preparation and excitement for the following day. I woke up at an ungodly hour to ensure I was ready by the time she awoke. And sure enough, as soon as she batted her beautiful eyes, there I was to give her the warmest hug, and wish her the happiest of birthdays. As she continued to wake up, I called in the troops for the festivities to begin.

My father, sister, grandmother, uncle, aunt, and I entered her room with balloons tossed her way, her beautiful brown eyes gazing at the multicolored air-filled wonders pouring down all over her, lighting up the room with her scintillating smile.

After our family's rendition of "Happy Birthday," British Catherine made an entrance.

"Hear ye, hear ye," I proclaimed, trying my hardest to remember the proper intonations of my favorite *Downton Abbey* characters, and not first scene Eliza Doolittle from *My Fair Lady*.

"It is of Royal Decree that the Queen, Her Majesty, Ana M. Young, shall receive thirteen presents to commemorate her Royal 63rd Birthday! To commence the celebration, please proceed to the dining room chamber," I instructed, reading off a small gold notebook from Buckingham Palace that I had fortuitously saved from my time in London.

And so, starting from my mother's room, I had created a path using two hundred long-stemmed white roses, her favorite flowers, leading to the dining room, where the rest of the thirteen presents were set. I will never forget the blooming awe on my mother's beautiful face as she seemingly floated down the stairs at the sight of such wonder. It was as if she had found her own secret garden, sweetening the house with a perfumed floral scent.

"Gift #1: Flowers; The Queen has received two hundred white roses, handpicked from the gardens of Windsor," I recounted, as if part of the Royal Court.

By Windsor, I mean FlowersDirect.com.

Once my mother approached the chamber, her smile continued to grow exponentially at the sight of all the shimmering silver, white, and gold presents, wrapped and adorned in the stateliest fashion. Nothing but the best for the Queen, of course. (I hope you too are reading this with a British accent, which I cannot seem to shake from my head as I write).

And so, the presentation of gifts continued.

"Gift #2: Crown Jewels; The Queen has received a special commemorative birthday crown secured in the Tower of London," I described, displaying a gold crown I purchased (quite realistic if I do say so myself) from Amazon, encased in The Container Store's finest clear acrylic box.

"Gift #3: Crucifix; As Head of the Church of England, The Queen has received a Royal Crucifix from the University of Notre Dame."

This gift was the first to make my mother cry, due to the emotional connection of the story behind the cross.

"Gift #4: Royal Robe; The Queen shall receive a royal robe to offset London's wintry months in the cold corridors of Buckingham Palace."

My mother loved Pottery Barn robes, so I purchased a white one to add to her impressive and fluffy collection.

"Gift #5: The Gift of Language; The Queen shall receive French lessons once a week to expand her proficiency in the language of diplomacy, as well as stimulate her mind with the best French tutor from Oxford."

This gift, presented in the form of a French Larousse dictionary, involved paying for weekly lessons since my mother always wanted to learn the language.

"Gift #6: Royal Satchel; The Queen has received a royal satchel, made from authentic British wood from the shores of the Cayman Islands."

And by Cayman Islands I mean Urban Outfitters. My mother loved a light brown wicker purse I sported on occasion, so I bought one for her to match.

"Gift #7: Memory Captured; The Queen has received a moment captured in time to warm her heart and lift her spirits."

This gift also sparked a wonderful reaction because it was a photo of a spectacle that is hard to come by: a giraffe sitting on the ground. One time when we were staying at the Animal Kingdom Lodge, a Disney hotel with a manmade savannah in the middle so you can see wildlife from your room, we saw a sedentary giraffe. As another example of her great optimism, my mother never forgot this moment and kept mentioning how much she wanted a framed photograph of the occasion. And thus, I made her wish a reality.

"Gift #8: The Gift of Music; The Queen shall attend the Royal Opera House in Covent Garden for a classical music concert presented by the London Symphony Orchestra."

This gift was presented in a little piano with a hidden note outlining the specifics of the event: Brahms' Piano Concerto No. 1. About a month later, the four of us attended the concert, and my mother acted as I do when I am at Disney during Christmas: giddy with glee and inspired by music.

"Gift #9: Royal Rouge à Lèvres; The Queen has received her favorite shade of lipstick to wear, a color fit for a Queen!"

To hit on all her favorite things, I purchased the lipstick my mother wore almost every day, knowing she could always benefit from having another in possession. Naturally, I wore it often as well.

"Gift #10: Teatime; The Queen has been invited for unlimited teatime. Lady Grey would be most pleased!"

As part of my plan to constantly bring her joy and laughter, I would often host teatime to allude to the happy memories of our previous London adventures. These experiences involved me dressing up like Mary Poppins or Cinderella, setting the table with fine china and hints of English culture, displaying shortbread cookies and jams for consumption, and of course speaking in a British accent all the while. The gift for her birthday was presented by means of a box of Lady Grey tea, her favorite kind along with Earl Grey, serving as a promise for the continuation of such fun gatherings.

"Gift #11: Royal Handkerchief; The Queen has received a handmade royal handkerchief to wipe away any and all tears."

One of the side-effects of the chemotherapies was overactive tear ducts, which caused my mother's eyes to water at all times of day. Thus, I purchased her a dainty lace handkerchief from Brooks Brothers so she could have on hand to combat the effect.

"Gift #12: Preservation of International Relations; The Queen has received a signed letter by the President of the United States, lauding her efforts in all matters, foreign and domestic."

Because my mother loved receiving the letter from the President, she yearned to have it framed due to the powerful message and incredible gesture. I therefore took it to her favorite local framing shop, where of course, the salesclerk knew her by name. Set in a golden frame, the letter still stands, reminding each of us of the powerful message her example set.

"Gift #13: The Gift of Words; The Queen has received a card most true! Happy Birthday My beautiful Mommy! God Save the Queen!"

This was the final gift. A delightful, *Downton Abbey* themed Papyrus card in which I exposed the innermost dwellings of my heart and soul.

After the thirteenth present, and English Catherine finally took a backset, my beautiful Queen continued to open the rest of her presents. What followed was brunch at the Oxford Exchange, her favorite brunch venue, dinner in St. Petersburg, Florida, where we both consumed duck à l'orange and blue cheese salads and ended the night with a classical music concert in the Palladium.

I have never spent more money, time, thought, or passion for one birthday as much as I did on this one. And I am so glad I did. There was nothing I would have changed, nothing I would have added or discarded. It was the perfect day.

**Task 5:** Album

My beautiful, gregarious mother had the opportunity to have lunch with Ann Romney, Cindy McCain, and other political dignitaries during the 2012 campaign season in Tampa. A piece of my mother's conversation with Mrs. Romney was shared with the Tampa Tribune, quoting her later that evening, "We need a new beginning. He is our new beginning."

Completely elated to have appeared in the newspaper, my mother began to use the phrase "new beginning" beyond the context of politics. It became a quasi-motto of hers to address ventures and newfound hope in the inevitable twists and turns of life. And thus, this phrase inspired the album.

One of my beautiful mother's favorite activities was to take photos to capture the memories of her wonderful existence. Not only did she appreciate her own impressive outward beauty, but also, she acknowledged the finiteness of life which led her to repeatedly exceed her phone's iCloud storage. But more so than just capturing moments of time, I wanted the album to serve as a vessel of hope, underscoring the silver linings of an arduous journey, highlighting the good in her "new beginning." That is, all the moments from Task #1, i.e., every occasion of ceaseless smiles and reminders of strength made its way into that fateful album, given to My Queen on her alleged last day of chemo.

And so, after all the tears and hugs brought about by combing through the collection of memories highlighted in the album, my beautiful mother reached the last page. There was an envelope with a letter, bringing the final task to completion.

**Task 6:** Letters of Life

My amazing mother opened the envelope, and proceeded to read the following message:

> "My dearest Mommy,
>
> As the album has helped demonstrate, your 'New Beginning' has been an incredible journey of life, love, and faith. We have laughed, we have sung (sometimes in several languages), gone to P.F. Chang's, Lightning games, and so much more. We have also unceasingly received beautiful words of encouragement, gifts, and actions by those around us. These overwhelming displays of affection towards you led me to an idea, an idea that will be brought to fruition as you continue to read this letter.
>
> In celebration of your last round of chemo, I've compiled a collection of letters from individuals who love and admire you.
>
> This project, that I have so dearly called "Letters of Life," has been one of the most fulfilling and awe-inspiring ventures I've ever embarked on. You, my dearest mother, are loved beyond comprehension. Every single person has not only lovingly accepted my proposal of writing you a letter, but has gone above and beyond, highlighting the incredibly special person you are and the impact you've bestowed upon all.
>
> Please enjoy reading these words of encouragement and triumph, and bask in the glory that is to be you, my beautiful Mommy, My Queen that shall reigneth forever. May they serve as a beautiful reminder of just how much you're loved.

I will love you with my whole heart today, tomorrow, and forever.

Catherine A. Young"

In preparation for the day in which I would present said letters, letters to serve as ammunition to boost her morale in times of need, I asked close family and friends to write a few lines of encouragement as she battled her ferocious cancer. I will never forget those who did, nor could I ever dismiss from my mind the level of enthusiasm and kindness behind every person's response. The love shown was truly overwhelming. After collecting over eighty letters, I made sure to place every note, sent by mail or electronically via email or text messages, carefully in a gold envelope of its own, each with the phrase "Letters of Life" written across the middle. I then placed the letters in a beautiful gold box with a big white bow, fit for a Queen.

And so, almost every day for a year, we would read a letter or two to foster feelings of hope and love.

As soon as my mother's brain cancer started spreading more rapidly, and her verbal communication and comprehension started diminishing, I knew in the depths of my soul that time was no longer on our side. And so, we finished all eighty plus letters, except for one: mine.

I wanted to leave mine last because I thought it was only fitting to end the project by having the orchestrator share her final piece. In addition, as the youngest sibling, born in December, and having a last name start with the letter Y, I always believed in the power of going last. Furthermore, I wanted to wait for the right moment, a day in which my mother showed more clarity so she could truly feel the words I had to share.

But I knew time was running out. So, one day, on the tenth of May, Guatemalan Mother's Day, as my mother lay in bed for an afternoon nap, I rushed to my room, grabbed the final letter, and proceeded to read,

"My dearest Queen,

How do I even begin to write this letter? How can I ever express the kindness in your heart, the knowledge in your mind, and the spirit in your soul that has unceasingly inspired me from birth? How do I put into words the love I can feel towards a single human being, a person so special and so extraordinary, that God so chose to undergo this test of strength and courage, this trial of faith and heart?

Everything happens for a reason. Especially this. You have been chosen by God, My Mommy! The power of prayer, love, and hope has come out in its truest form because of this, transcending all beliefs and moving mountains. After today, you have climbed your mountain, you have surpassed all odds, and you have set an example to any and all individuals that are blessed to know you.

You are everything the world needs and more. You are the perfect example of inner life, the exquisite pairing of grace and perseverance, the beacon of hope for the power of optimism. You are my everything, my inspiration for all, my partner in dance, my voice of reason, my classical music enthusiast, my fellow Francophile, my biggest cheerleader. You have given me everything. My beautiful existence and way of perceiving the world are all directly correlated with the love you've shown me and the support you've never stopped providing.

I hope this letter, as well as the others, serve as a constant reminder of the incredible person you are and the countless lives you've touched.

May God bless you forever and always my beautiful Mommy! I am so proud to be your daughter and I thank you with all my heart for my beautiful existence. Every wonderful thing I've done, and every incredible feat I'm going to do, has been and will always be a direct reflection of you.

With my greatest love and admiration,

Your Catarini Pini"

  Upon reading it, my face damp with tears, my sweet mother gave no indication of understanding, and proceeded to speak nonsensical phrases regarding my sister's whereabouts. My heart broke. I wanted to crumble. But I stayed in bed with her, holding her beautiful hand as she fell asleep, as we had done before. And somehow through the sadness, I kept the faith that I could one day properly relay the contents of my letter.

  About a month later, we met with her oncologists at Moffitt one final time. They gave us the news we never wanted to hear: we were going to lose her, and soon. I remember amidst receiving this harsh reality, I did not fall to the ground. I kept walking. I kept wanting to complete tasks to not deal with the flood of emotion boiling within me. I went to work and gathered my things, letting my superiors know I would be taking a few weeks to spend the final moments with My Queen in Guatemala. Tears kept flowing down my cheeks as an unstoppable stream as I said my goodbyes to my coworkers. Little did I know what incredible gesture I would find as I checked my email later that afternoon:

> We wanted to return the favor and gift your mom with her very own poem. We love you so much <3
>
> Ana Young, The Marvelous Mom
>
> Ana Young, sweet Ana Young; Could anyone ask for a better Mother?
>
> It's time to write her a love letter, from your GMI sisters and brothers.
>
> She's a valedictorian, she beat those jealous girls at the race
>
> And no one can compare to her beauty and grace
>
> You know Ana Young loves you when she gifts you individualized birthday cakes
>
> Her Halloween spreads were made for 40 when only 6 would partake
>
> She's a marvelous mom, celebrated with flowers she would buy
>
> Decorating a Christmas tree with mini cereal boxes 7 feet high
>
> Ana Young has lived a life that is worthy of a book
>
> Giving back to others and fighting valiantly against cancer, giving it all it took
>
> And even in her most challenging days, she still put others first
>
> Making her nurses and doctors smile when she felt the worst
>
> Your Mom's life is full, and her spirit is strong
>
> And although we've only met a few times, her impression on our hearts will be life-long
>
> And one of her greatest gifts? She has spread her spirit to you

> Her wit, poise, light-heartedness and caring are in you, too
> So, as you take this most honorable journey hand-in-hand with your mom
> Know that we support you and love you in all the days to come

 My beautiful friend, Jenna Hernandez, took it upon herself to compose an incredible poem for my sweet mother, truly capturing her essence and providing me with an unbelievable sense of comfort at a time when I needed it most. Just as I had written poems for several individuals in the office, granted some of them were roasts, the gift of words was everything I could have asked for in this poem of my very own. It was upon reading Jenna's poem that I knew I had to go through this, but I knew I was not alone, giving me the strength to continue moving.

 There were preparations to be made, things to pack, my mother's final outfit for her eternal resting place to pick out. And somehow, I kept walking. I was able to finish all tasks, knowing full-well I could not stop. I knew I could not break down now because I had to equip My Queen with only the best, even in her final moments of life.

 Just before it was time to go to bed, amidst all the chaos of my family members making phone calls, crying, tending to my mother's needs, and packing, my mother and I shared a few minutes alone as she sat on the couch, her eyes closed, and breathing heavy. I sat there with her, kissing her soft cheek, and embracing her beautiful body. I proceeded to thank her with such feeling for everything, I promised her I would live my life according to the values and principles she instilled in me, and I gave her my word that I would finish this book to share with the world the powerful story of her magnificent life. We were to leave for Guatemala the next morning, and an unsettling thought flew into my head: tonight would be the last night my beautiful mother spent in our wonderful home.

 And so, that final night, I asked my father if I could sleep in the same bed with them, just as I had done so many times before as a little girl. Fearing he would say no to spend one final night alone with his beautiful bride, my father turns to me and with a soft smile responded almost immediately, "Of course." I still thank my incredible father for that gift of allowing me to relive my favorite part about growing up, spending the night alongside My Queen.

It all started feeling so real. I knew now more than ever this was the end.

And thus, the following morning, we flew back to My Queen's childhood home, with all my family members already there to greet us. We spent the last few days catering to her every need, soaking up every smile and moment when she would open her beautiful eyes. Sometimes she would even respond.

There were four moments of clarity I will never forget. The first occurred on the second day we arrived. My cousins wanted to take my sister and I to have lunch at a nearby café. Usually, I would be the first to say yes because I love spending time with them. But this was different. I knew I could not leave My Queen's side.

So, I went back to her room, and asked, *"Me puedo meter a la cama con usted?"* (Translation: Can I get in the bed with you?")

She responded, with the most beautiful smile, *"Ay si!! Qué alegre!"* (Oh yes!! How fun!")

My fate was sealed. I stayed home and napped with the biggest smile on my face alongside My Queen, holding her hand and sharing in another Hallmark movie moment.

Another moment of clarity occurred randomly when I was lying in bed beside her. She turned to me, and said very matter of factly, *"I'm fine, usted tranquila."* (Translation: You relax).

This struck me to my core. My mother in her infinite strength was trying to shield us from pain and worry, even during the unimaginable hardship she was experiencing. Another example of how she never strayed away from her *Life is Beautiful* parenting.

The third moment occurred towards the end, during which she opened her eyes and saw me in her favorite pjs of mine (which I had, of course, bought her a matching set), She said then, with the biggest, most angelic smile on her face, "How are you?! *Qué elegante!*" (Translation: How elegant!)

This was very Mom. She never failed to notice when you leaned in on the side of elegance.

That night, I received the last hug. I will never forget it. It was a perfect embrace of love and tranquility. The joining of two of the world's most loving hearts, founded upon great respect and mutual friendship. The impact it had, the power it spread, and the quickness with which it left will forever reside in my memory. I remember crying so much at the joy that was mine to be held by my beautiful Queen once more, but also sobbing at the sorrow of knowing I would need to eventually withdraw. In that hug, I let go but would forever hang on.

I remember as a little girl, sitting on my beautiful mother's lap while she reclined on our white wicker rocking chair and read me the story of *The Princess and the Pea*. I remember pressing my cheek against her soft chest, listening to her heartbeat more so than to the story she told. In that very moment, I remember acknowledging the great gift I had in my mother's embrace, and how lucky I was to be there. It was the most perfect place in the whole world, and I had unlimited access to it. Just me and My Mommy, her beautiful luscious hair, her soft warm skin, and the sweet comfort in hearing her heartbeat as she held me close.

Oh, how I will never forget those wonderful hugs. I am convinced that without my beautiful mother's displays of affection and her example, I wouldn't know what love is, what it means, what it can bring about, how it can transform, and cause you to grow, achieve, and dream. How it can lift you, inspire you, change you in a way unimaginable, even to yourself.

This was the hug. The promise that her work as a mother was finally complete.

The last moment of clarity was during the final hours.

As her oxygen level became dangerously low, and her blood

pressure sparse, I gathered the courage to articulate the words, "You'll always be with me, right Mama?"

She responded, "*Si mi muchachita.*" (Translation: Yes, my daughter).

And so, as she was nearing the end, my father, sister, grandmother, and I all around her, we heard her say faintly and with great effort, "I lo…"

I know she wanted to say *I love you*, but her body was too compromised for her to articulate another word again.

My mother's resilience and fight within her never ceased, even at the end. Despite the lack of breaths, my mother continued to press on. We thought she was passing for about eight hours. But that was mom. She was a fighter, and never gave up.

But, of course, God had another plan. At 7:26 p.m. on June 26, 2019, with her entire family around her, and with me at her side holding her beautiful hand, she took her last breath and made her way to Heaven.

Later that evening right before heading to sleep, I was having tremendous difficulty coming to terms with what had just happened.

Crying uncontrollably, I turned to my sister who shared the following thought, "Mom doesn't have cancer anymore. She's finally ok."

The peace I felt upon internalizing those words transformed my tears into joyous blubbering.

In between breaths, I started repeating, "That's all we've ever wanted for her. That's all we've ever wanted for her."

"Plus, Cath," my sister continued, noticing the success of her comforting words. "Mom has finally met her best friend of all these years, she has finally met the Virgin Mary. She's with Mary!"

I started crying even harder. I was overwhelmed with happiness in realizing these beautiful truths. My beautiful Queen was finally cancer-free, in Heaven, accompanied by beings she worshiped. My sadness, although not completely shaken, was lessened with the solace of this profound veracity.

The following morning, my eyes puffy and heart heavy, I proceeded to get ready for the onerous day ahead. It was the Queen's burial, and I knew I had to look my best. Because my mother made a significant effort day in and day out when we were little girls to ensure our appearance met a superior condition, I knew her funeral could be no exception. No matter how much I wanted to just stay in bed with a pint of ice cream and box of Kleenex, it was the day in which we would honor the Queen for her great deeds and tremendous life. It had to be perfect, tailored to the highest of standards with which she lived her life.

And it was. Even in death, my mother's influence invoked the arrival of what seemed like half the population of Guatemala City. I have never seen so many people for one person's service.

Her sarcophagus was submerged with thousands of splendiferous flowers; it was as if my beautiful mother had her own secret garden yet again.

At first, the thought of meeting with so many people felt like the last thing my aching heart yearned for. However, the more I met with her friends and family, the more I felt at peace. It helped me to hear how truly beloved she was by so many, even by people I had never met before. She was regarded by the masses as nothing short of spectacular, solidifying that which I already knew. In addition, most people told me I looked exactly like her, seeing in me the same light and strength that characterized My Queen. I began to feel her inside of me, that her baton had been passed, and her seeds had been sowed. I felt this great honor and pride in being the daughter of the incredible Ana M. Young, realizing now more than ever that I was destined to carry out her legacy.

Halfway through the service, my cousin Jordi played a video compilation of moments of her extraordinary life. Created a few days before, this video made its way to My Queen's eyes just before she passed. Since my beautiful mother loved photos, this was the perfect remembrance. We are forever grateful to Jordi for such a wonderful expression of love.

Despite the insurmountable pain I felt, I knew I had to share the overflowing love and admiration I possess for my sweet mother. And so, at her burial, with a great tremble in my voice, I stood up in front of family and friends to share her *Letter of Life:*

> "Quiero compartir unas palabras de mi adorada madre, and Queen, en inglés, primero porque así me puedo expresar mejor, y segundo, porque a Mommy le encantaba el inglés, siempre diciendo que le parecía muy elegante y distinguido. (Translation: I want to share a few words about my beautiful mother and Queen, in English one, so I can express myself better and two, because my mother loved the English language, always saying she thought it was very elegant and distinguished.)
>
> My mom's life was like a beautiful piece of classical music. Every encounter with her left a lasting impression, just as a beautiful orchestra does with its majestic symphonies and grand concertos.
>
> However, what music and all the words in the world cannot accurately convey is the kindness in her heart, the knowledge in her mind, and the spirit in her soul that has unceasingly inspired me, and so many, from birth. How do I put into words the love I, as well as so many people, can feel towards a single human being, a person so special and so extraordinary, that God so chose to undergo such tests of strength and courage, such trials of faith and heart? The power of prayer, love, and hope has come out in its truest form during this time through all her close friends and family. So, thank you from the bottom of my heart for the support you've all shown her.
>
> You have climbed your mountain, My Mommy, you have lived an extraordinary life, and you have set an example to any and all individuals that are blessed to have known you. You are everything the world needs and more, the perfect example of inner life, the exquisite pairing of grace and perseverance, the beacon of hope for the power of optimism. You are and will always be, my everything, my favorite person, my inspiration for all, my partner in dance, my voice of reason, my classical music enthusiast, my fellow Francophile, my biggest cheerleader. You have given me everything. My wonderful life and way of perceiving the world are all directly correlated with the love you've shown our beautiful family and the support you've never stopped providing.
>
> To my Tricky Bird y adorada Abuela, thank you for raising such an incredible individual who never settled for anything less than the best in all she did. To my beautiful sister, thank you for being her Margita, caring for her, and loving her with every ounce of your being until the end of her extraordinary life. And to my wonderful

father, thank you for loving My Mommy so deeply, showing Margaret Anne and I what an incredible spouse and partner of life truly means. Our gratitude for everything you've done for our beautiful mother will never cease, nor will our love for you.

May God bless you forever and always, my beautiful Mommy! I am so proud to be your daughter, and I thank you with all my heart for my beautiful existence. Every wonderful thing I've done, and every incredible feat I'm going to do, has been, and will always be a direct reflection of you.

I love you, My Mommy."

Never have I ever felt a moment more difficult and more powerful all at once. There I was, standing next to my mother's casket, reciting the last words to the greatest human I will ever come to know. The beauty of this moment also stems from the incontestable fact that my Letter of Life was finally complete. I was both humbled and honored for the opportunity.

It was all so surreal. As my mother's beautiful body was laid to rest, my entire family gazed in peaceful sorrow, thankful for our great faith that this was not the end. It was merely her *new beginning*.

As is custom in Guatemala, after the sarcophagus is set in its eternal resting place, members of the deceased's immediate family will line up so each attendee can extend their condolences. I will never forget one man in particular, Herman, an individual I had never seen before.

As he went in for a hug, he shared with me the following thought, "I didn't know your mother well, but through your words, I felt as though I had, so thank you for sharing what an extraordinary woman she was."

Tears were streaming down both our faces at this point.

He continued, "You see, I knew your grandfather, and what you said about how your mother loved the English language, resonated with me because your grandfather used to say it as well. She was a special lady who will truly be missed."

This comment hit me with another thistle of tears, as I knew this fact about my grandfather, and felt his presence closer than ever before. Knowing my mother was once again reunited with her favorite person in the afterlife alleviated my anguish, as I thanked Herman once again for his sharing.

And so, as the service ended, and everyone left my mother's earthly resting place, our family gathered in Abuela's house to continue keeping each other company. Once there, we all shared stories, laughed, cried, and even sang along to my cousin's guitar playing. I will never forget this moment during which the memory of my mom transformed mourning into music. There we all were, smiling through our sadness, singing along to one of my mother's favorite songs, "Leaving on a Jet Plane," and I couldn't help but think about how my beautiful mother had done it again: spreading her light and joy, even beyond the grave.

People often dwell in the reality that I, a twenty-four-year-old bachelorette, was too young to have lost my mother. There have been days where I also find myself mourning the "what-could-have-beens" that accompany this reality: the first encounter of My Queen with the love of my life subsequently resulting in an extensive interview to prove his worthiness, wedding dress shopping that would have resulted in a downpour of tears and an excessive consumption of Kleenex, the spectacle of introducing my beautiful mother to her granddaughter bearing her very name, the list goes on. But in these moments, I am comforted by the following thought: my mother deserved to have our full and undivided attention during the last moments of her life. Her dedication to her family during her existence left a pay it forward to the universe. If I had already been married with kids, I would not have had the time or mental capacity to cater to her every need, to sing her songs in various languages, to watch movies with her and hold her hand, to spend the quality time God graced me with until her very last breath. So, whenever I think about those pesky "what-could-have-beens," I am reminded of this beautiful truth, because it was the greatest gift from God to have smiled so much, laughed so much, and cared so much for my beautiful angel during the entirety of her most extraordinary life.

About four months after my mother's passing, we ran into one of her oncologists, Dr. Susan Minton, while at Mass at our local parish. Because she decided to stop practicing medicine during the time my mother's cancer was slow growing, she didn't know my mother had reached her eternal resting place. Thus, she reacted as most do upon hearing of her death: speechless and overcome with emotion.

Dr. Minton, with a grace and empathy so becoming of her, gathered herself and shared an observation with me, my father, and sister, "Here was a woman that was full of cancer, and you could not tell in the slightest. It was amazing how she carried herself."

This message, so powerful and true, fizzled in my head with memories of My Mommy. Here was her doctor, admitting the extremity with which the cancer pervaded her beautiful body. How was this possible when she never broke down, never conceded to notions of negativity, and never perished in her resolve to keep living an extraordinary life? Only one possible explanation: a miracle.

I am forever indebted to the people and places that supported me and my family during this journey. To all the physicians, nurses, oncologists, radiologists, technicians, and all members of hospital staff who cared for my mother, thank you. Just as tears are insufficient in capturing sorrow, words could never portray the gratitude I possess towards each of you. Thank you for prolonging the life of my dear mother for twenty-three extraordinary years.

To all my coworkers, friends, and family members, thank you. I would not have survived this chapter if it were not for the undeniable support and tremendous acts of love you showed me in my moments of greatest need. Thank you, a million times over.

My beautiful Queen's journey through life was exquisite. Her existence provided an extra dimension to all who knew her, beautiful in form, perfect in perspective, and profound in spirit. I know with all my heart that God and the angels opened the gates of Heaven with the sound of Handel welcoming my mother into the arms of the Virgin Mary. I look forward to the day I too will be reunited once again with My Mommy so we can laugh and dance just as we have done so many times before. But until then, I will live my life as My Queen would have wanted me to be: unafraid, full of knowledge, full of faith, full of love, and never, *ever*, giving up.

    I am my grandfather's granddaughter. I am aware of the ever-present notion of excellence, the living embodiment of the value of hard work, the personification of resilience, strength, and gratitude for the gifts of everyday life.

    I am my grandmother's granddaughter. I am a disciple of placing family at the forefront of all, guided by God our Father and the Most Holy Blessed Virgin.

    I am my father's daughter. The daughter of a US Air Force Officer, graced with a love of country and inner strength to keep pursuing, keep feeling, keep dreaming.

    I am my sister's sister. An avid believer that the essence of all people is good, an advocate in the power of humility, always desiring to offer kindness to others.

    I am a compilation of many incredible people, the byproduct of events, interests, and personalities that have led me to how I perceive the world.

    But most of all, I am my mother's daughter: filled with great faith, long-lasting hope, and extraordinary love for the joys of today and the irrefutably certain magnificence of tomorrow.

    My mother's love is so powerful that it extends beyond the grave, still inspiring me, still leading me towards a happiness unfamiliar to most. I have never known and will never come across a more beautiful and extraordinary life. Here is your new beginning my beautiful Mommy. Rest easy, as you have excelled in all. The wisdom you have possessed and the love you have shown will never cease.

    I love you, My Mommy.

*My mother and I praying at the Grotto at the University of Notre Dame.*

CHAPTER ELEVEN

# The Miracle

*Believe.*

**DECEMBER 15, 2011**

*I* have always believed in the afterlife. I have always known in my heart the existence of Heaven, the presence of angels, the blessings bestowed upon us by God, our Father. However strong my faith, I have never been more convinced of the great beyond until living this story.

The Saturday after my beautiful mother's journey to Heaven took place, two of my cousins, Felipe and Martín, decided to take my sister and I to breakfast. Upon our return, our flustered father spoke softly, yet poignantly, "I have something very important to share with you."

Upon hearing these words, my heart sank. I merely sat down in the nearest chair and gazed at my father. He began to read off a piece of paper held in his trembling hand.

"Thomas called," he started.

Thomas is our neighbor in Antigua. From San Luis Obispo, Thomas fell in love with Guatemala and decided to spend most of his time living in a beautiful house in the old capital. He is a very intelligent, charitable, and selfless man, a man whom my mother always viewed as her guardian angel due to his acts of kindness and thoughtful gestures. These include offering over three hundred Masses for my mother's recovery and the portrait of her as an angel in his home.

Upon hearing that Thomas called, I was expecting some sort

of worldly gift, like traditional Guatemalan bread he would deliver on occasion. I would have never suspected how much more valuable the gift truly was, or whom the gift was actually from.

The story my father told was the following: on the third day after my mom's passing, Thomas proceeded with his routine of attending daily Mass. That Friday, he decided to attend Mass at the church where my parents got married. He found it comforting and surprising that the priest presiding over the Mass was Padre José Contrán; comforting because he was my mother's favorite priest due to Padre Contrán's saint-like presence, and surprising because it was not his usual time to give Mass. Regardless, as they were great friends, Thomas happily joined the congregation and took his place near the front as the altar server and sacristan.

About halfway through the Mass, during the time when everyone prayed the Our Father, Thomas heard a voice:

> **"This is Ana. This is Ana. This is Ana. I am at peace. I have no pain. Tell Bill and the girls that I am sorry I didn't have the opportunity to tell them how much I love them in the last period of my life."**

"Thomas heard Mommy's voice. She sent us this message," my father shared through a broken voice, shaken by impending tears.

Upon hearing this, I immediately started to weep. It was as if every Mass, every rosary, every prayer, and petition had reached its point of actualization. I was struck to my core in a way far beyond what any 26-letter alphabet could encapsulate. Simply put, I felt peace. I knew her death in this life meant a birth in the next.

My family, upon witnessing my hysteria, shuffled about to find *Passiflora*, an anti-anxiety medication used for moments of great stress. But I knew I didn't need a pill or tablet. What I needed was to fully wrap my arms around the all-consuming happiness flooding uncontrollably from my body. I had just heard the most astounding, earth-shattering news, pointing to the undeniable fact that there is a God, and my mother is with Him in Heaven.

The next day, we all headed to Antigua to meet with Thomas and hear the story firsthand. Now Thomas, as he recounted the story, made the disclaimer that he has never been a drinker, nor has he ever taken any drugs, so he could not have been under the influence of any kind. He states simply and very matter-of-factly that he heard the sweetness of my mother's voice "as clear as a bell."

"The message was as clear as it could be. Your mother said:

> **'This is Ana. This is Ana. This is Ana. I am at peace. I have no pain. Tell Bill and the girls that I am sorry I didn't have the opportunity to tell them how much I love them in the last period of my life.'**

After hearing those words, I just started to cry. So much so that Padre Contrán looked over. I not only heard the words; I felt the message."

A few things are extraordinary about this communication, solidifying my belief in its validity. First, my mother always referred to herself as Ana when conversing with Thomas. Secondly, Thomas never referred to my father as *Bill* or to my sister and I as the *girls*. This phrase was very much only used by my beautiful Queen. In addition, Thomas never knew that my mother could not communicate well in the final weeks of her life. So, Thomas could not have known when delivering this message. Other reasons to believe include: it happened three days after her death (three is a holy number in Christianity), during a Mass dedicated to her soul, given by her favorite priest, in the house of God where she got married, a short distance away from her childhood home, and in her favorite city in the world… The perfect time and place for a miracle if you ask me.

Thomas proceeded in recounting what happened, "The reader next to me just looked at me. Padre José didn't say a word either. And then I saw your grandmother on the side with a glow around her, with a halo, dressed in black. The whole thing didn't take three or four minutes."

He paused, and we began asking questions regarding how he could have seen my grandmother, who was with us in Guatemala City at the time this occurred. Perhaps it was my beautiful Queen, embodied as her mother in an act of maternal symbolism. Perhaps it was the Virgin Mary personifying my mother's transition from being with her earthly mother to joining her Mother in Heaven. Perhaps there is some other spiritual reason beyond the mental aptitude of human comprehension. Regardless, Thomas describes it as another gift my mother threw in.

He continued, "Your mother sent you girls that message as she passed to the Great Spirit. Now, why she sent it through me, was maybe because we were in the Mass for her, or maybe because Padre José was giving Mass. Maybe she chose me because she thought you were too emotional to receive the message. Don't know. I was not part of the program. I was just a messenger. I tried calling you that night, but you didn't answer, so I repeated the words over and over in my head all night so I wouldn't change anything."

Another reason why it is believable is the fact that Thomas received the message. Thomas, my mother's guardian angel, is a faithful servant of God. It is also worth mentioning that Thomas never cries or shows excessive emotion, especially during the solemnity of Mass, so the fact that he did certainly insinuates something earth-shaking occurred.

Maybe God also chose him because his faith was shaken due to his supposed "unanswered" prayers and "futile" Masses for my mother's healing offered daily for over a year. But I am certain, that because of all those prayers and Masses, my mother's life was extended for far longer than the norm. I believe sometimes we ask God for miracles, but we almost always do not know their full extent. But I know God grants them every day, perhaps in ways different than what or when we expect. In my beautiful mother's case, I know it was the prolongment of her extraordinary life, as well as this awe-inspiring gift: to hear her message from the Great Beyond.

"Whatever God's plan is, I don't know," Thomas continued. "But, at least, look what your mother left behind. She left behind two educated, smart, intelligent girls, with these wonderful memories. A friend of mine ten years ago had a brawl with his mother and never settled it. Another friend of mine, his mother died at ninety-six and left this world with this unsettled negativity. Your mother left this world with this glow! This glow of positive love and feelings for you. I wanted the opportunity to sit down with you and tell you so now you can go on with your lives with that peace in your heart, knowing that's how your mother left this world. And that God gave her the opportunity to tell you."

My beautiful Queen certainly pulled a "Can I speak with your manager?" but this time the manager was God and the request far more improbable than asking for any coveted table by the fish tank. But as with all things founded in faith, nothing is ever impossible.

Losing my dearest mother will always be the hardest thing I'll have to do. When you lose someone with so much light and life, you can't help but feel the night that much deeper. I cannot begin to quantify the pain I felt when I held her hand during her last hours, when I prayed with my family during her last moments, when I heard her last breath marked by my outward cry, or the months of continuous weeping generated by the physical pain of losing someone so precious. A grief so deep, not even tears were enough in capturing the sorrow.

And even with great faith, there are these moments of great sorrow. But when I find myself in such moments, I take comfort in the following words: It's ok to feel. It's ok to hold the grief close to your overflowing eyes and hollowed out breath. It's ok to feel the night deeply and dread the following days to come. It's ok to let the emptiness of a love so powerful consume you. It's ok because it's the only way. It's the only way to get better, to start healing, to carry forward in this life. This grieving experience, so poignant and pervasive is, as with all things, transient… It will pass. The sadness inevitably subsides. Each day brings a new understanding, a new sunrise to follow each sunset. And then, one day, the thought of tomorrow becomes less paralyzing. You suddenly realize the strength God bestowed upon you, a strength you possessed all along. You will press forward, and you will rise because you remember... you remember the miracle of Mom.

# Portfolio

*My parents' wedding in 1991.*

*My grandfather, sister, my grandmother, and I in our Tampa home in 1995.*

*My father carrying my sister, and my mother carrying me soon after I was born in 1994.*

*My sister and I with "Chicken" in 1997.*

*Me, my mother, sister, and Millie in our Tampa home for Christmas in 1994.*

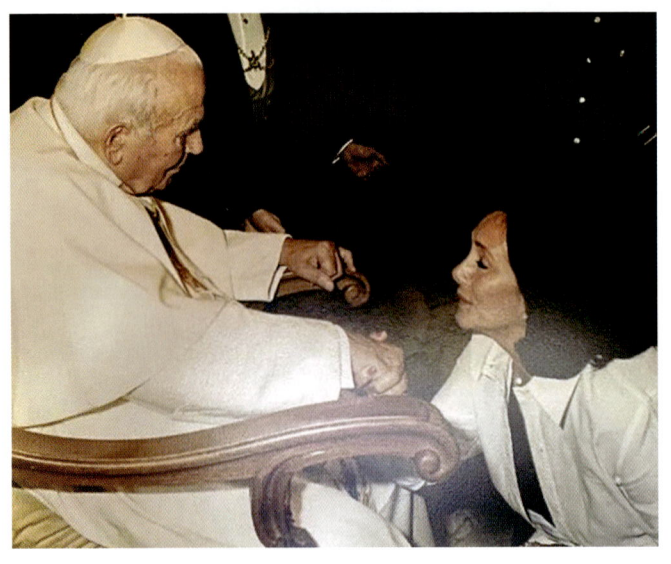

*My mother kissing Pope John Paul II's hand at the Vatican in 2002.*

*My grandparents, parents, sister, and I riding a Surrey bike at Disney's Boardwalk Inn in 2003.*

*Abuelo and my mother in Abuelo's study in Guatemala City in 2008.*

*My mother, Abuelo, and Abuela for my grandfather's check-up at Moffitt in 2009.*

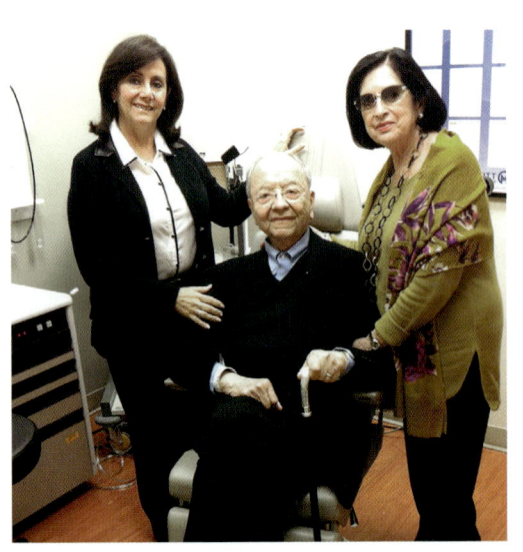

*My mother and sister with George and Laura Bush in 2014.*

*The Solares Camacho family
in Athens, Greece in 2008.*

*My beautiful mother for Christmas
in our Tampa home in 2013.*

*My mother with Our Lady of Fátima in Fátima, Portugal in 2017.*

*My mother and I at the Magic Kingdom for Mickey's Very Merry Christmas in 2017.*

*My mother and I during her 62nd birthday at Bern's Steak House in Tampa in 2018.*

*My father, sister, mother and I at one of our favorite restaurants in Antigua, Guatemala in 2018.*

*My beautiful mother and I
during one of her chemo treatments in 2018.*

*My mother's tree on Notre Dame Avenue
in front of the Morris Inn.*

*My mother's tree plaque
at the University of Notre Dame.*

*The 13 gifts for my mother's 63rd birthday.*

*Found a pot of gold in
Dublin, Ireland in 2015.*

*Left to right: Margaret Anne, Tía Olguita, Abuela,
my mother, Tío Joey, me, and María Olga (cousin)
in Antigua, Gautemala in 2019.*

*My mother painted as an angel
in the upper left corner in Thomas's home in Antigua.*

*My mother looking out from her dream condo
in St. Pete Beach.*

*My mother, sister, and I enjoying breakfast in Antigua, Guatemala in 2003.*

*My beautiful mother with her two girls.*

*Standing in front of my mother's golden leaf after its dedication at Holy Cross-Immaculata in Cincinnati on February 13, 2021.*

*Ana Margarita Solares, top right, with her three siblings and parents.*

*My mother enjoying a piña colada at St. Pete Beach in 2014.*

*Ana M. Young*

# Afterword

Who are we but mere transients passing through this life, gathering experiences, establishing connections with those around us, making an impact both large and small?

My beautiful mother, wow! She certainly made an impact in this world. I hope this book will help carry that impact forward, providing others with the hope that we all too, can live an extraordinary life, founded in faith, fostered in love, and always believing in the power of possibility.

One beautiful day in 2016, as I traversed the charming streets of my quaint Italian neighborhood during my semester abroad in Rome, I became overwhelmed with a need to unload the innermost understandings of my soul. And thus, at the first café I stumbled upon, I bought an espresso, sat down, and wrote out what I consider to be a comprehensive overview of my major life beliefs, inspired by my beautiful mother's example:

> Life is hard. It's a challenge. There's always a mountain to climb. Always a river to cross. Always two roads to choose between. But life is incredible. It's a gift that bears many fruits, all we have to do is acknowledge the complexity of the mind and harness our ability to morph our perceptions.
>
> It's all about perspective. About choosing to alter one's point of vision for the better. Of course, this is easier said than done. But just with anything, it becomes easier with time. It becomes a habitual practice of accepting situations, of looking forward to the peaks, rather than dwelling on the valleys. It becomes your way of seeing the world, not always as it is, but as it could be.

Being happy is not only a situational emotion, it's a way of life, a habit, an integral part of self. It's about knowing that the essence of life is good, with each life having a purpose, a meaning greater than we may ever realize.

I strongly believe God has a greater purpose for me. There is a reason why I am so blessed with so many opportunities, while throughout the world, others struggle for survival. My life's purpose, I believe, is to be kind to others, to show people how inner happiness can enrich life, how despite hardship, happiness will prevail and guide us back to attaining self-fulfillment.

There absolutely is a reason why I am on this Earth. I believe my life has been so beautiful, so full of opportunities—such as my experiences abroad, traveling with my family, having another world in a different country, my education, family, friends, trips to Disney, everything. I have even found beauty in the failures, the heartaches, the separations, the stressful situations... all because of my core life beliefs.

If there is anything I believe, I believe there is a God who is smiling upon me each and every day, protecting me and infusing my spirit with the strength to keep going, to keep working, to keep smiling, to keep dreaming. I know He loves me, I feel it when I wake up, when I see the goodness in others, when I take in the beauty of his creation by merely walking down the street, when I smell the crisp air and bask in a blanket of sun or feel raindrops on my skin. I feel Him in the wind through the trees, in the clouds of the sky, in the awe-inspiring bodies of water that seem to transcend all, taking away with it worry and pain to the ends of an unceasing horizon.

That which solidifies my faith in God is the incontestable fact that everything, every situation in life, every tribulation, every great achievement, every daily occurrence, happens for a reason. God is guiding us through life, still allowing us to decide which route to take, but helping us along the way to realize our greatness, to find our purpose, to discover true love.

The other most certain belief of mine is love. I believe love can reach into the depths of our soul and ignite a flame that makes us feel more alive than ever before. Whomever I end up with, I know I will love them deeply, incandescently, and with all my being.

One of my favorite quotes from one of my favorite movies:

> "Love is passion, obsession, someone you can't live without. I say, fall head over heels. Find someone you can love like crazy and who will love you the same way back. How do you find him? Well, you forget your head, and you listen to your heart. And I'm not hearing any heart. Cause the truth is, honey, there's no sense living your life without this. To make the journey and not fall deeply in love, well, you haven't lived a life at all. But you have to try, cause if you haven't tried, you haven't lived."
>
> – William Parrish, *Meet Joe Black*.

I have loved, I have been loved, and I have lost love. All have taken a toll on my heart, but I will never lose faith in its power, in its ability to transform, to inspire, to heal.

In my twenty-one years of existence, I have cultivated these beliefs through a wide array of experiences. I will never stop trusting in their power, for I believe they will hold true even as I begin to progress further into adulthood. All I can do now is learn from the past, thrive in the present, and hope for an even better tomorrow.

Life is beautiful. It's a mystery. It's a string of events waiting to unfold. It's a journey with bumps, both large and small, but nevertheless, a journey worth taking. You will end up where you're meant to be, with whom you're meant to be with. God loves you, happiness will endure, and love will triumph.

I mention this because I hope this book will help you discover your core life beliefs, as my mother inspired me to develop mine. Her incredible example and story brought substance to these few short lines. She gave the words more meaning than letters setting strings of syllables. She made the words come to life, elevating off the page, and waltzing away in rhythmic perfection.

To part? Never. To love, always. To cherish, forever.

I am going to make it count for you, my beautiful Queen.

I love you, My Mommy.